LIZ ATTWELL (1960-2019) taught at Michael Hall
School, Sussex, for fourteen years. She read English
Literature at Exeter University, followed by teacher
training in Secondary English and drama with Dorothy
Heathcote at Newcastle University, where she was
introduced to Process drama and the concept of handing
'the mantle of the expert' back to students. She taught in a comprehensive
school and in 1986 took the Foundation Year at Emerson College, Sussex,
followed by Dawn Langman's Speech and Drama course and a stint of
teaching at Edinburgh Steiner School. During the 1990s, Liz raised her
three children and helped to save and restructure Tablehurst Biodynamic
Farm in Forest Row. She completed a training in Education at Emerson
College and began her work at Michael Hall, where she helped to introduce
Continuing Professional Development and Theory U change management,
whilst researching the interface between mainstream technique and the
epistemology that underpins Waldorf Education for an MA in Creativity
in Education at King's College, London.

A DROP OF LIGHT

EDUCATING FOR THE A-HA MOMENT

LIZ ATTWELL

Edited by Josie Alwyn, Annie Attwell,
Emma Attwell and Catherine Fenton,
with contributions by Josie Alwyn and Catherine Fenton

RUDOLF STEINER PRESS

Rudolf Steiner Press,
Hillside House, The Square
Forest Row, RH18 5ES

www.rudolfsteinerpress.com

Published by Rudolf Steiner Press 2020

A catalogue record for this book is available from the British Library

ISBN 978 1 85584 575 6

Cover by Morgan Creative
Typeset by Symbiosys Technologies, Visakhapatnam, India
Printed and bound by 4Edge Ltd., Essex

CONTENTS

FOREWORD

Three days before she died, Liz Attwell, my mother, chaired her last editorial meeting—a final chance to transfer her thoughts and discoveries to us, the swiftly formed group of colleagues, friends and family who were to bring this book to publication. Having received the terminal diagnosis of cancer a year earlier, her inspirations and ideas came thicker and faster as her time approached, building on her years of research and insight on the significance of a-ha moments and the urgent need for a renewal of education. Many of these ideas were first written up during her Creativity in Education MA, the essays from which now form the basis of the first three chapters of this book.

As her quest led her deeper into what was actually taking place during a-ha moments, Liz became increasingly aware of the wide-ranging implications of these moments of inspiration. She presented her ideas at conferences, training days and lectures. She had dreams of travelling to schools across the world, helping to bridge the gap between Steiner and mainstream education. In fact, she had just become the Education section coordinator for the Anthroposophical Society in Great Britain when she received her initial diagnosis of breast cancer.

Our editorial group has come together to give Liz's ideas a future life. Josie Alwyn has written the final chapter of Part One, having worked with Liz for years at Michael Hall Steiner school, bringing to bear her deep knowledge of anthroposophy and teaching English. Catherine Fenton worked closely with Liz also at Michael Hall, both as a student teacher and colleague, and wrote *A-ha! Why You Should Never Teach Your Students Anything*, a practical guide to implementing Liz's teaching ideas in your own classroom—first published as a booklet—which is included here. Annie Attwell, her daughter, has created the diagrams while I have edited and proofed the manuscript and held the overall organization of the project.

Our thanks to Ian Botting for his diligent referencing and support of Josie in her mammoth task of bringing together Liz's most complicated ideas in the final chapter. Finally, our heartfelt thanks to everyone who inspired and worked with Liz: friends, family, colleagues and especially students.

Emma Attwell

Introduction

Towards Progressive Education

There *is* a battle raging for the soul of the human being and education *is* the frontline. Concepts such as Artificial Intelligence and Transhumanism add urgency to the situation. A truly human education for the twenty-first century needs continuous forging.

Ken Robinson has clearly delineated two positions in education—traditional v. progressive. I have found both kinds of teacher in every school, Steiner schools included. Which you are is not a matter entirely of the philosophy you espouse: but of the way you experience your own relationship to the world. The difference is in the underlying being of the teacher and the 'medium is the message' in this case.

In Robinson's characterization the traditionalist sees the child as an 'empty vessel' into which the teacher's job is to download information. The progressive teacher, on the other hand, sees the child more in terms of a plant that unfolds from within, according to its own intrinsic organic needs. This changes the role of the teacher to one of providing the right conditions; soil, sunshine, water. These positions are actually describing two different ways of relating to the world. Both have validity. But the linear, logical, traditionalist viewpoint is dominating, to the detriment of humanity and the planet. As teachers, working on balancing these two sides in ourselves is our responsibility and our privilege.

The experience of dualism is natural in our time, it sees the world as separate and it threatens to lead us into the destruction of the planet and our humanity. In our time this consciousness needs to be balanced and 'wrapped around with' a participatory or unitary consciousness that brings a wholeness back. My experience is that progressive teaching can engender this, bringing joy to pupil and teacher alike.

As the largest independent school movement in the world, and spanning one hundred years of development, Steiner education has a contribution to make. However, to make that contribution it needs to come into conversation with other progressive teachers around the world, and to continually examine and renew itself to meet the needs of current society. This book is brought out with this in mind.

It is in three parts—in reverse order: Part Three—an intimate depiction of my process as I move progressively deeper into my understanding of a-ha moments and their significance, recorded in my diary, kept in my bedside table over a seven year period.

Part Two is written as a 'how to' guide by Catherine Fenton with springboard ideas for teachers to use in their lessons.

Part One gives the rationale. The first chapter of this describes a lesson in which a class I taught rose from secondary consciousness to participatory consciousness in a single lesson—and my analysis of how that came about. The second looks at why, with every good intention, traditional teachers are only addressing a small part of the soul of a child, and that there is 'another way of knowing' which they are missing. The third investigates the archetypal experience of the act of knowing and its implications for creating self-actualizing capacities in students. The fourth draws together the overarching concepts, the spiritual/psychological background to this experience, with far-reaching implications for the future.

As I write, my oncologist has given me a month to live. I am so grateful to the group that have formed around me to collate my work.

PART ONE: THE ESSAYS

Chapter One

PRACTISING GOETHEAN SCIENCE WHILST STUDYING ENGLISH LITERATURE OR, RIDING THE MAGIC CARPET

[In which Liz describes a breakthrough English lesson where the students took off into free and independent insight, and examines why it took flight; takes issue with the no-drama rule in English lessons at Eton, introduces Ken Robinson's 'Rationalism v. Romanticism' debate, outlines the overlooked importance of Goethe's methods of observation; seeing in Robinson's plea the need for a new unification of science and art in education, and finishes by asserting that the resonance between Goethe and Robinson could allow Steiner schools and their unique insights to contribute to the conversation about the 'New Renaissance.']

What caused AS English Literature at Michael Hall to take off like a jet-propelled rocket at 11am on 18 October 2012? Why did it happen and how do I do it again?

It was like walking together through a door marked 'summer' (sorry, another metaphor). One moment I was with eight AS students worried about their first coursework essay and the next we were all electrified, with complex concepts and connections about *A Midsummer Night's Dream* tumbling out of each one of us. We had achieved lift-off. Ironically, the ninth member of the group was away debating the issue of legal highs in London while back in the classroom we were experiencing our own learning high. How had we got here?

I had been quite concerned about this group. They were open, lively and willing: but, at first, their thinking about literature lacked muscularity. Their ideas had little deep insight or analytical rigour; they seemed to expect me to supply information rather than really engage with the texts at anything more than surface level.

They were the first group I had taught to have had controlled assessments in their English GCSE, writing their assignments in class under timed conditions rather than in their own time at home as hitherto. In meetings with their GCSE teacher we both wondered whether this had something to do with it. It had meant that their teacher had taught more to the test than before. Now, facing independent written coursework in their first term of A-levels they looked to me to supply answers. I looked back! As each student had chosen an individual essay title, I was not in a position to do the work for them.

What to do? We had used all the teaching tools in my bag in the six weeks of term so far. I had introduced comedy as a genre. We had played different comedy skits. We had read the play; lifting it off the page as much as possible with improvised acting. We had created tableaux expressing key concepts, written re-creative responses and practiced analytical writing. Now they had to choose a topic and write their essay. Yet still they did not feel ready, and I had to agree. I told them they just had to start.

After they had begun I had one last idea. We'd had a good discussion about the way that the ending is not as simply comic as it seems on the surface. I felt there was still more to uncover, so, although we were starting a new text, I set four critical extracts about the ending of Shakespearean comedies as a starter activity.

I split them into four groups of two to read and discuss one extract and then brought them back together to share them. One extract quoted four lines from *A Midsummer Night's Dream*:

Jack shall have Jill,
Naught shall go ill:
The man shall have his mare again,
And all shall be well.[1]

Seeing those four lines, on the spur of the moment I split them up again to analyze one line each. It was when they came back from this that the lesson took off.

It began because H started to quote lines from the play. H would be regarded as the least academically able at English in the class. We agreed that he would go forward to study A-level on the basis that he might take two years over AS. He is enthusiastic about literature and wants to be an actor. He has a very good memory for lines from plays. H saw a connection between his line and Puck's entrance at the end of Act Five saying:

I am sent with broom before
To sweep the dust behind the door.

Everyone tuned into the fact that 'the dust' was all the unresolved issues in the play.

Suddenly each person, with the individual topic they had done, became an expert in their area. Everyone could see implications for their topic. Each was contributing from a unique perspective.

H, buoyed up by success, saw connection after connection. He produced original concepts whole, and others, more analytically-minded, separated out the parts and explained them. At one point H was cooking up another idea and I instructed everyone, 'Pens poised, the oracle is about to speak!' Another pupil who was encouraging an idea out of H imperiously stopped me from interrupting with a raised hand. I humbly waited. When the process was over she typed it up while two boys (usually too cool to care) ran round to see it going up on the screen.

I looked around my classroom. We had become a fully-fledged learning community. Everyone in the room was totally animated. Each was playing a role that drew on their particular strengths. Some were accurately recording, others analyzing and yet others were producing original ideas.

Of course we never got beyond the starter that day. The whole hour and a half was devoted to feverish debate. The lesson had to stop for lunch but the discussion went out into the corridors. My canteen lunch was punctuated with students coming up to test new ideas.

Pupils carried on all afternoon; explaining to peers what had happened. One pupil reported that she went round the canteen to all the Year Eleven's saying 'Do AS English Literature'!

It had a profound effect on their essay writing. All of them went home and scrapped their work so far, rewriting the essay entirely. All except T, who just tacked the new ideas on in the second half. I could clearly see the 'join' and duly instructed him to rewrite the first half to bring it up to the level of the second.

Next week I asked them to record their experience in response to five questions: how did it start; what did you learn; what did you feel; what made it work; was there anything you did not like? Here are some of the answers. (I have explained how it started based on their accounts.)

What Did You Learn?

'There are many different interpretations of aspects of the play. People elaborated on someone's comment/explaining it.' . . . . . . M.
'We were building and connecting ideas as a group.' . . . . .J.
'Group brainstorming is extremely effective.' . . . . T.
'We went much more in depth than I thought was possible—there were countless intriguing insights. Ideas were easily developed and escalated.' . . . . A.
'That debates and ideas are the best ways to spark imagination. Knowing something really well and discussing it with a group you know really well uncovers all the underground intricacies.' . . E.
'Hearing others' opinions made me challenge mine ... that one hour of inspiration is far better than six of individual reading.'. R.
'I usually like working on my own but I want to do this again and my hand is shaking with excitement thinking about it.' . . . . . C.

How Did You Feel?

'Like the whole play had suddenly opened up/unfolded and shown
us all its secrets/meanings.' . . . . M.
'The whole play opened up, exposing layers, it revealed itself and we
made the links.' . . . . .J.
'Very excited, interested.' . . . . T.
'It was very exciting and intense ... we could have carried
on for ages since we were on such a roll.'. . . . . A.
'Like I'd drunk a litre of coffee!' . . . . E.
'Inspiration.' . . . . R.
'I felt really hyped up and like my brain was firing faster
than usual. I forgot Shakespeare was dead!' . . . . C.
'I really want to do it again. It made me realise I wasn't dumn (sic).' H.

What Made It Work?

The general consensus was that knowing each other so well was a
major factor. Most of the group have been in the same class for most
lessons for several years; three for eleven years!

What Didn't You Like?

'I would have loved to spend the afternoon writing the essay.' . . . .J.
'Not enough time to write everything down.' . . . . .M.
'Needed more time.'. . . . . T.
'We didn't get the chance to turn energy into productivity.' . . . . . E.
'It went too quickly and I wanted to write my essay there and then.' . R.
'The lesson ended'☹ . . . . C.

I can assure you that while my pupils are generally positive about
my lessons these are not, unfortunately, reactions that I am used to! I
include them, not just because I am inordinately proud of them, but to
show that the students also recognized this as a significant event and
because some of the wording they use points, in my opinion, to aspects
of the learning experience which are significant for understanding it.
I will explore these aspects later. Suffice to say that The Lesson, as we
have come to call it, marked a sustained improvement in classroom
dynamics. Team working improved, eye contact with me improved,
and a new commitment to the subject and its possibilities was defi-
nitely discernible.

So, what went right? Could the fact that I was doing a module on *Performance Arts in the Classroom* and incorporating some of its methods have had an impact? One speaker on the course would have answered a pretty emphatic 'No.' Simon Dormandy, Head of Theatre at Eton College, firmly presented the case that drama belongs in putting on plays and nowhere else. In his essay 'The Arts and Creativity—integrating performing arts based approaches across the curriculum', he states that although his pupils in theatre are up and active and despite the fact he teaches English Literature in a state-of-the-art rehearsal room 'I *never* get them up on their feet.'

He elaborates:

> Eton is a highly selective school. All the boys I see have passed a rigorous series of written exams [...] they are already experts at absorbing, challenging, reshaping and debating ideas solely through the medium of words. Most of them can sit through hours of lessons and not drop dead with boredom or climb the walls in frustration.

He continues:

> I believe their time is better spent wholly in the realm of language: the medium in which they will have to communicate their ideas with the utmost rigour, rather than one, which, however rich and interesting it might be, is, in my experience, far less productive of useable, high-grade, critical ideas. It's not that I don't think that there are insights available to readers if they engage their bodies and senses; it's just that I don't think this is the best way to learn the beautiful and essential art of critical analysis.[2]

Simon goes on to explain, 'I think there is a meaningful integrity to the ways in which a discipline is studied and taught and that the approaches evolved to suit the study of a particular discipline are probably the ones best suited to its communication.' As a result, Simon says, he is not 'knocking at other teacher's doors' to persuade them to use cross-curricular methods and he notes that they are not knocking at his. He does acknowledge that these cross-curricular arts might have merit in the teaching of 'less able' students, but the implication is that if Eton's teachers aren't using them it is because for the top echelons it is not useful.

It is a strong opinion and an act of bravery to state such a case on the course. Perhaps that is why he chose to read his essay out for half an hour rather than to give a talk. It is even more striking when one takes into consideration that before he became a teacher he acted in the Royal Shakespeare Company and Cheek by Jowl (one of the most physically innovative theatre companies of the last decades). He is anxious that we 'don't get the impression that I don't value drama as an educational medium. I happen to think that it is the most powerful medium I know for educating the whole person. I just think that its educative power is at its strongest when it is being pursued for its own sake.'

Was I just wasting my pupils' time with all the drama exercises that I did? After all, it *was* in discussion of 'beautiful and essential' critical ideas that take-off occurred. Perhaps Simon is right.

Simon's situation makes an interesting comparison with mine. He has acting experience and is Head of Theatre at arguably the most eminent public school in the land. I am the English teacher at Michael Hall Steiner School, sometimes known as 'the alternative Eton'! We are not a selective school, though we are private at present. We do know about excellence, however, getting consistently high results and winning the Good Schools Guide award for English Literature results over three years in 2009. Whilst not having Simon's acting experience I did train with Dorothy Heathcote, a pioneer in the drama in education movement, in my PGCE at Newcastle during the 1980s.

So, Simon versus Liz! Eton versus Steiner education! Product drama versus process drama! 'Rigour' versus creativity!

Rigour seems to have the upper hand at the moment. Michael Gove has made it clear that he wants a return to 'traditional' methods in education. In fact a battle is being waged between Rigour and Creativity in education. In April 2011 Gove, as Education Secretary, criticized schools for a 'lack of rigour' in not studying pre-twentieth century classics in literature, teaching British History or giving students 'a rooting in basic scientific principles' (*Daily Telegraph*, 23.04.11).

I do not wish to attack Simon Dormandy, who is clearly a practitioner to be respected. However, I do think that we can see some aspects of his essay which put him on the side of what Ken Robinson would call the Rationalist attitude as opposed to that more allied to the Romantic movement. It lies in his implicit acceptance that the linguistic-mathematical measures of intelligence are the only valid ones, that a student's main aim is to sit still and absorb hours of lessons whilst not 'climbing the walls', and that (perhaps most breathtaking of all) methods of assessment have an intrinsic and meaningful integrity with the subject.

In his book *Out of Our Minds* (2009), Ken Robinson tracks the arising of this polarity between Rationalism and Romanticism. The Middle Ages, with its earth-centric view and unquestioning belief in God saw mind and matter, Robinson says, as a unity. The discoveries of Copernicus, Galileo and Newton changed that. In particular Newton in his *Principia* (1687) envisaged the universe as a clock. This mechanized vision of the universe lends itself to a negation of the inner life of the human being. Matter becomes all we can be sure of: we are on the route to seeing mind as a by-product of matter.

Meanwhile, in philosophy, Descartes (1596-1650) was building a rational edifice in which nothing could be taken on trust. His empirical method looks for provable relations between cause and effect. Only what can be proven is admissible. As Robinson says 'Rationalism and Empiricism opened up a "fissure" between the arts and sciences. Science increasingly had no use for the inner life of the human being.'[3] This paradigm shift underlies the accepted mode of modern thinking. Robinson pays tribute to the 'incalculable' advances that scientific materialism has contributed to, but adds:

> There has been a heavy price too, not least in the schism of the arts and science in the domination of the rationalist attitude, especially in the forms of education to which it has given rise.[4]

He summarizes this effect as having 'driven a wedge between intellect and emotion' and leading to the 'imbalanced development' of millions of people. His critique is lengthy and damning and he argues that as a culture we are desperately in need of rebalancing.

Robinson does say that there was a reaction to the Enlightenment. This took place in the late eighteenth and early nineteenth century and took the form of Romanticism. It was carried forward by the powerful work of artists and musicians, he mentions in particular Beethoven, Schiller, Wordsworth, Coleridge, Byron and Goethe. Robinson says that 'in contrast to the Rationalists, the Romantics were focused on the quality of human experience and on the nature of human existence.'[5] These artists, while keeping a sense of transcendence alive in the arts, seem to have had little influence on the modern scientific mindset which Robinson holds responsible for distorting education.

Ken Robinson summarizes the Rationalist worldview thus:

> the powers of logic and deduction are the true hallmarks of independent thought; true knowledge is objective and independent of cultural values and personal feelings. A rational mind is developed through absorbing the various bodies of knowledge, the main roles of teachers is to transmit bodies of knowledge.[6]

We can hear an echo of this, I would suggest, implicit in Simon Dormandy's essay.

In contrast Robinson characterizes the 'natural' or Romantic view as one in which children are unique, with innate talents and sensibilities. Education should draw this out, 'engaging feelings, physical development, moral education and creativity.'[7] In this tradition he cites educators such as Johann Pestalozzi (1746-1827), Friedrich Froebel (1782-1852), Maria Montessori (1870-1952), Rudolf Steiner (1861-1925), Carl Orff (1895-1982) and John Dewey (1859-1952).

Robinson then makes an impassioned plea for a New Renaissance; a way of synthesizing science and art, thinking and feeling. In all the literature that I have read, one name has been mentioned that I feel has not been fully appreciated for the role that he could play in Ken Robinson's New Renaissance: that name is Goethe.

Johann Wolfgang von Goethe (1749-1832) is mentioned by Ken Robinson as a leading artist of the Romantic Movement. He is generally known as a giant of German Romantic literature, the author of *Faust* and along with Schiller, Germany's nearest equivalent to Shakespeare. Less well known is the fact that he was a keen scientist who made important discoveries for his time and 'considered his scientific research and writing, diligently pursued through five decades, to be his most significant achievement.' In his introduction to Goethe's *The Metamorphosis of Plants*, Gordon L. Miller explains that Goethe echoed Spinoza's vision that 'spirit and matter, soul and body, thought and extension...are the necessary twin ingredients of the universe and will forever be. Therefore he believed that the most perfect instrument to understand both matter and the ideal was the human being him/herself.'[8] This corresponds with Robinson's assertion that 'the capacity for personal judgement is probably the most sensitive instrument a scientist has.'[9] Robinson continues, 'discoveries in science often result from unexpected leaps of imagination ... many of the great discoveries were made intuitively ... scientific understanding is the product of the creative mind.'[10] Goethe, who was horrified by the separation of mind and matter that he saw science in general and Newton in particular enacting, was consciously working in a way Robinson would recognize in the 1780s!

Goethe worked at developing what he called a 'delicate empiricism'; a method which I think could act as an archetype or model for all modes of enquiry, and which achieves the union of science and art in education that Ken Robinson is signalling that we so desperately need. Gordon L. Miller expresses Goethe's intention so beautifully and appositely that I will give the whole paragraph from his introduction:

> In order for us to comprehend not only the outer material aspect of natural things, Goethe discovered that we correspondingly must employ both the eyes of the body and the 'eyes of the mind', both sensory and intuitive perception, 'in constant and spirited harmony.'

He coupled rigorous empiricism with precise imagination to see particular phenomena as concrete symbols of the universal principles, organizing ideas, or inner laws of nature. Starting from sense perception of the outer particulars, Goethe's scientific approach seeks the higher goal of an illuminating knowledge from within. This way of knowing—from the inside—is rooted ultimately in a harmony or identity between the human spirit and the informing spirit of nature, wherein 'speaks one spirit to the other.'[11]

It is my contention that such an approach can also be used in literature. Just as it was possible for Goethe, as he put it, to 'read the anatomy of an animal like a text' so it is possible to read the 'bones' of a text until the play, novel or poem begins to live in you.

Goethe's method can be adapted for use in the classroom. The first step is to apply rigorous observation of the phenomenon. This differs from conventional science which tends to form a hypothesis and then test it through experiment, often by separating the phenomenon into its constituent parts and analyzing them. Goethe laid a strong emphasis on studying the phenomena in context. With the plant this takes the form of studying it where it grows, over a long period of time, and really coming to know the plant's form and structure. In literature this is analogous to the stage at which we are reading the text, simply establishing exactly what is going on, and then moving to a comprehensive understanding of its constituent parts within the form and structure of the text.

The second step is 'exact sensory perception.' As Goethe puts it 'we initially see the different leaves as discrete steps in a process', however, he says that to understand the growth of the plant, an intrinsic unity, we have to think the growth sequences through time (Goethe did it both forwards and backwards). Each leaf or part of the plant becomes a snapshot in time of a continuous process. When he did this Goethe experienced, as Miller put it, 'the dynamic inward archetype' or as Goethe put it the Urphenomenon. In my study of literature I lay great emphasis on the structure of the text. The scenes of a play, chapters of a book, or the verses of a poem can be seen as analogous to the leaves on the plant. If students reach the point of being able to really think through the structure of the text forwards and backwards then there can come a point where the text lifts off the page and becomes a 'living entity' in the room. Then all those sitting around the table can see it as a reality. This is the point that I am always searching for in my teaching. The text becomes like a three-dimensional structure within which we can see new connections which we can communicate to each other. At this point subject/object dualism is overcome.

When this happens we have reached the third stage of Goethe's method in which the Urphenomenon unfolds itself to the inner eye. This is the feeling that my students are expressing in response to the question 'What did you learn?' Note that I asked them to think about the process they underwent rather than the information they gleaned for their essays. Comments like 'the whole play suddenly opened up/unfolded and showed us all its secrets/meanings' really convey this moment.

Other comments that build on this impression are that there were 'countless intriguing insights', and that 'layers were exposed and the play revealed itself.' Notice that the play has taken on a life of its own.

The fourth stage is one in which the participant responds to the phenomenon from within. This response is part of the conversation that arises between the Urphenomenon and the participant and is often linked to a willed response on the part of the participant which is free and at the same time intrinsically moral. This stage was somewhat blocked in my lesson by the lunch bell, a reflection of the fragmentary nature of a school day. The pupils' responses to the question 'What didn't you like?' reflects the depth of their engagement in the moment and their frustration at not being able to respond in writing their ideas down fully. They make comments such as 'I would have loved to spend the afternoon writing the essay' and complaining that they did not 'get the chance to turn energy into productivity.'

Now listen to Ken Robinson's description of creativity and the process of finding yourself in your element from his book, *The Element: How Finding Your Passion Changes Everything*. Robinson defines the process of creativity 'as the process of having original ideas that have value.'[12] He adds that 'you can think of creativity as a conversation between what we're trying to figure out and the media we are using'[13] and 'creative thinking depends greatly on what is sometimes called divergent or lateral thinking, especially on thinking in metaphors or seeing analogies.'[14] We ourselves, says Robinson, are the medium for our creative work which 'reaches deep into our intuitive and unconscious minds and into our hearts and feelings ... there is far more to our minds than the deliberate processes of conscious thought. Beneath the noisy surface there are deep reserves of memory and association, of feelings and perceptions that process and record our life's experiences beyond our conscious awareness.'[15]

Robinson goes on to describe the implications of this new access to creativity:

> The recognition of common creative processes in the arts and the sciences has led to a wide range of collaborative projects and to the early dawning of what may prove in our own times to be a New Renaissance. It is a Renaissance based on a more holistic understanding of human consciousness; of the relationships between knowing and feeling; and of all that we think and feel is part of the creative process of making sense of the world around us and of the worlds within us.

Goethe was dismayed by the separation of art and science in his time. As Miller says, he embodied his belief that science and poetry/literature, in both of which he excelled, can be united. 'People forget,' he said in his

Botanical Writings, 'that science had developed from poetry and they failed to take into consideration that a swing of the pendulum might beneficently reunite the two, at a higher level and to mutual advantage.' Goethe was an early exponent of the Creativity in Education movement's New Renaissance!

Now, bearing in mind my students remarks and Goethe's method please read this digest of Ken Robinson's characterization of the experience of being in the Zone, the place where we are most in our element. He begins, 'to be in the Zone is to be deep in the Element, the meeting point between natural aptitude and personal passion.'[16] Robinson says that when we are in the Zone 'our minds merge with our bodies and we feel ourselves drawn effortlessly into the heart of the Element.' The Zone gives a sense of 'freedom and authenticity' and is 'centred in our true sense of self.' In it, 'time moves more quickly and more fluidly.' It is a 'meta-state' where:

> ideas come more quickly, as if you are tapping a source that makes it significantly easier to achieve your task. There's a real sense of ideas flowing through you and out of you; that you're in some way channelling these things. You're being an instrument of them rather than being obstructive to them or struggling to reach them.[17]

In the Zone 'people become instruments of their own expression.' The Zone 'can be associated with physiological changes in the body—there may be a release of endorphins in the brain and of adrenaline through the body. There may be an increase in Alpha Wave activity and changes in our metabolic rates and in the patterns of our breathing and heartbeats.'[18]

Pretty much all these details are recognizable in the responses of my students: the sense of ideas flowing easily ('ideas were easily developed and escalated'); the feelings of exhilaration; of having drunk a litre of coffee ('we were on a roll'); the shaking hands; the feeling that Shakespeare was still alive! So, that is what happened at 11a.m. on 18 October 2012—we entered the Zone together!

Why did it happen? I think it happened because I used enough of a Goethean approach and that Goethe was tapping into the same source on which Robinson and the creativity movement are drawing, so the creative exercises helped to get us to the Zone.

How do I do it again? How, as a teacher, can I replicate this? By its very nature this was a unique and unrepeatable event. However, Ken Robinson does point out that 'finding our Element often requires the aid and guidance of others'[19] and he does follow that with a description of an inspirational teacher of his wife's. As he says, 'when mentors serve this function—either turning a light on a new world or fanning the flames of interest into genuine passion—they do exalted work.'[20]

He sees four roles of a mentor. Am I being fanciful to see in those roles an echo of Goethe's method? The first role is *recognition*. This seems to me to be predicated on rigorous attention to the phenomenon; in this case, the student. As Robinson says 'I don't know of any test or software program that can make the kinds of subtle, personal distinctions that differentiate an interest from a potential burning passion.'[21] So here, again, the human being turns out to be the best instrument.

The second role of a mentor for Robinson is *encouragement*. A teacher has a responsibility to create an open, safe learning environment where it is OK to take risks. Robinson says that mentors 'lead us to believe that we can achieve something that seemed improbable or impossible to us before we met them … they stand by to remind us of the skills we already possess and what we can achieve if we continue to work hard.'[22] This is the sort of persistence needed to arrive at the point that a subject can take off.

The third role of a mentor is *facilitating*. A teacher's job is to design tasks that make the learners actively engaged so that the subject becomes their own. Here creative techniques of process drama are very helpful to support the students make an active relationship to the text.

The fourth role is *stretching*. In my group I felt that we had not yet really plumbed the depths of what they could do, so I designed one last activity which turned the key. Robinson says 'mentors push us past what we see as our limits.'[23]

In *Out of Our Minds*, Robinson follows his call for a New Renaissance with a description of human culture and its relationship to creativity. In the chapter 'Defining Cultures' he writes:

> We live in two worlds, the inner world of personal consciousness and the outer world of material consciousness. What we create in common is our culture.

He quotes anthropologist Clifford Geerts (1926-2006) saying 'all human lives are suspended in "webs of significance" that we ourselves have spun'. He continues, 'creativity is the process by which these threads are formed and it is in our interaction with others that they are woven into the rich fabrics of human culture. Creativity and culture are the warp and weft of human understanding.'[24]

I would like to take Ken Robinson's analogy of a textile further (note the link to a literary *text*). Steiner schools value community very highly indeed. Three of the students had been studying together for eleven years, some had been with us a shorter time and one was new. I had not taught any of them before. In our class, over six weeks, we had succeeded in weaving the warp and weft of a true learning community—a magic carpet.

In *Out of Our Minds*, an initiative by the Blue Man Group is described to found a school with a commitment to achieve a 'new kind of balance between rigour and enchantment' with a belief that both are essential in education. He quotes Chris Wink, a co-founder, as saying:

> On a metaphorical level, the traditional model of education is that children are freight cars and the school is a grain silo. It fills each kid up and then moves them down the track. We're creating a launch pad where kids are the rockets and we're just trying to find the fuse (ibid. p. 292).

So, to disastrously mix my metaphors from my title again; in the service of creativity—having woven a text-ile carpet out of shared Goethean observation in a true learning community, I lit the fuse and jumped onto the magic carpet to rocket with my students to the archetypal land of a midsummer night's dream!

Here might be a method in which Science and Art, so long estranged, could effect a marriage and engender the birth of a New Renaissance. Goethe developed his methods over two hundred years ago. Over one hundred years ago Rudolf Steiner edited his collected scientific writings. From Goethe's approach, Steiner synthesized an educational approach which has resulted in the largest independent school movement in the world, with at least 1,400 schools worldwide. Yet the Steiner School movement seems hardly in the picture as far as the Creativity in Education movement is concerned. The reasons why this may be are beyond the scope of this chapter. However, the resonance that I have found between Goethe and Robinson might mean that the conditions are now right for the insights that the Steiner School movement have been nurturing to emerge into the mainstream. Then Steiner schools could enter the conversation on the side of creativity and play their part in the New Renaissance.

Chapter Two

Two Modes of Thinking
and Steiner's *The Science of Knowing*

[In which Liz describes the dry, technical and exam-oriented approach to English teaching currently prized over 'meaningful learning'; outlines different teaching styles from 'technicians' to 'old grammarians'; looks more deeply into Ken Robinson's dichotomy between the 'traditional' and the 'natural' in education, introduces John Dewey's vision of progressive education 80 years ago, and his pre-emptive dismissal of Michael Gove, sets out Steiner's work with Goethe's theory of knowledge, and how this influenced his own epistemology, the foundation of his educational work; then lays out Steiner's own theory of perception and thinking in The Science of Knowing, his description of Intellect and Reason, how one takes apart and the other puts together again, describes Bruner's logico-scientific and narrative modes of thinking and ends by showing how Steiner's epistemology of creative inner activity confirms the Romantic worldview and can solve the imbalance of too much logos and too little mythos in education today.]

> *To say that all human thinking is essentially of two kinds—reasoning on the one hand, and narrative, descriptive, contemplative thinking on the other—is to say only what every reader's experience will corroborate.*
>
> William James—the epigram to *Actual Minds, Possible Worlds*.

Jez Butterworth's *Jerusalem* is a huge hit with my students. The hot theatre ticket of 2011, it was declared the play of the millennium and audiences camped out overnight for a chance to buy tickets. In a filmed interview with *The Guardian*, Jez Butterworth sees it as depicting a clash between Logos and Mythos:[1] 'We have too much Logos in our lives' he says, 'audience reactions show a desperate need for Mythos.'*

How does this dichotomy relate to English in education?

The Problem

On Tuesday 1 October 2013, the first day of my module *Notions of English*, I had time as I travelled up to London to buy a newspaper. On the letters page

---

* A useful reference for Mythos and Logos can be found in the Introduction to Karen Armstrong's *The Case for God* pp. 2-3

of *The Times* I read 'Narrow test-based education harms children.' It was a letter to Michael Gove, Education Secretary, from 198 children's authors and educational academics, including Malorie Blackman (Children's Laureate), Carol-Anne Duffy (Poet Laureate) and Michael Rosen. The letter expresses 'grave concern' at the impact of current developments of state education on children. I quote it extensively because it succinctly makes its case:

> The new national policies around curriculum assessment and accountability are taking enormous risks with the quality of children's lives and learning. Competition between children through incessant testing and labelling results in a public sense of failure for the vast majority. The drive towards ever-higher attainment in national tests leads inevitably to teaching to the test, which narrows the range of learning experiences.

They go on to assert that:

> Children are natural learners who deserve an abundance of new experiences ... childhood needs wide horizons, high hopes, confident expectation and absorption in the joys and challenges of meaningful learning.

This distinguished company calls on the Government to suspend its proposed changes and to seek 'a consensus of parents, teachers, academics, children's authors, business leaders, politicians and other public figures to decide on what we want for our children and how best to achieve it.' Their last sentence reads, 'arrest change and seek consensus on the future of education.' Ah, consensus; an elusive thing in the arena of education.

I arrived at King's and the first sentence I wrote down from the MA course leader Bethan Marshall's talk was 'What English, as a subject, is, has been contested since its beginning.' She outlined a battle between various points-of-view down the decades. I found myself on that first night in the midst of the issues as my peers and I discussed the various approaches. All except one of the participants on the course are in their 20s or early 30s and are newly-qualified teachers or teaching assistants. At 53, I am nearly twice their age. All seemed to be caught in teaching a curriculum dominated by spelling, punctuation and grammar (SPAG). All expressed discomfort with the dryness of the approach and expressed the desire to be more creative.

One said that she had tried to do similes and metaphors with a class but was told by a superior that this was too advanced and that she must go back to SPAG until her class 'got it' before she could think of doing something more 'creative.' However, she said, her group never seemed to 'get' the basics so she could not move on. Out of both my training in Newcastle in the 1980s and a lifetime of teaching experience I posited that their lack of progress was because children learn best when they are engaged in meaningfully creative learning embedded in a rich context. Another teacher countered that it is 'important, nevertheless, to be able to write a good business letter' and that as education was primarily there to give opportunities for employment those skills must be prioritised. I protested that children need something to communicate and that they will learn best to write formally if inspired to by imaginative engagement in a meaningful context. Bethan quietly added that all the research shows that I am right.

What worries me is that these newly-qualified teachers did not have a secure hold on this aspect of education: they were not clear that a rich imaginative relationship of the context in learning is vitally important to the progress of learning. I had been taught this in 1984 and Bethan seemed to indicate that a further 30 years of research had confirmed it. Yet here was a room of highly intelligent, gifted, newly trained teachers who seemed insecure in their grasp of this issue.

I was shocked. I am sorry to labour this, but if I knew this from a training in 1984 and the research has continued to reinforce this, how is it possible that in 2013 there is not a clear consensus, at least in the teaching profession?* If 198 children's authors and academics were asserting that 'meaningful learning' was paramount: but newly-qualified teachers, though expressing unease at the tasks they were asked to fulfil in the classroom, were not secure in this, how can we really expect 'parents, … business leaders, and politicians' to know it? What, I pondered, could overcome this split; how could we reach a secure consensus? Could there be a more important question for the welfare of children in education?

A Rough Guide to English: 'Technicians' versus 'Old Grammarians'

Bethan Marshall outlined an enduring and complex debate in the history of English teaching.

She drew on Matthew Arnold's concern that the human being was being distorted by 'faith in machinery'[2] and his dislike of what he saw as reductionist approaches to education in the Revised Code that was brought in during his school inspection years. The debate continued throughout the decades with the progressives having to defend their ideas against a tendency for government interference driven by concern about 'standards.' Bethan Marshall has identified five views of English teaching: Technicians, Pragmatists, Critical Dissenters, Liberal View, and what she calls Old Grammarians. She characterizes each group in a paragraph which I will quote in full for Old Grammarians and Technicians as they reflect each end of the spectrum.

---

* Indeed, in the years since this essay was written, the situation in schools has continued to rapidly deteriorate, to Liz's deep concern.

Technicians, are characterized by their 'desire to focus on the skills necessary to be good at English. They are likely to encourage pupils to study spelling, punctuation and grammar in order that they can become confident users of language. They are also keen to develop creative writing in order to encourage a more imaginative response to language.' The English Language end of things then.

As regards Old Grammarians, Marshall explains that, 'This group seeks to foster empathy, the imagination and enlightenment in the students which they teach. While they are not averse to the idea that some literature is better than others, they cannot have that choice imposed because teaching is about the book that will create the spark. It is about inspiration, which almost by definition cannot be imposed by government diktat.' The English Literature end of things then.

When Bethan Marshall surveyed teachers she found that they all could see themselves in one of these categories. Interestingly, she added, no one mentioned that they occupied more than one. Although this may have been because they felt that for the purposes of the survey they needed to fit into a category, it does point to being relatively happy with the characterizations. I took these categories back to the Waldorf/Steiner school in which I teach and showed them to my colleagues. They found them interesting, even beyond the English department. After pondering them, everyone I showed them to added, 'Of course, you need all five approaches.'

It seems to me that each position is the expression of a different definition, more or less conscious, of what a human being is. There is a spectrum being expressed here which begins with the technical side, which tends towards a materialistic/reductionist view of the human being. The spectrum then moves to a concern with the human being as a social being with the Critical Dissenters especially. The other end of the spectrum with Liberals and Old Grammarians is moving into a vision of the human being that relates to personal growth and would start to use terms such as 'the human spirit.' There would be an argument for this spectrum expressing a movement from the material, through a relation to the soul, and into a vision of the human being as spirit. But that would be beyond the possibilities of this chapter.

What I would like to point out though, and which *is* germane to this chapter, is that an Old Grammarian would naturally take into account all five approaches in some way, though having a leaning to the 'top' of the spectrum. But positions further down the spectrum, at the material/reductionist end, would tend not to address the needs of the human being implied further up. Therefore, it is vital that the image of the human being that is informing our teaching approaches is right or a terrible travesty will be visited on the children in our care.

The History of Notions of English

I am struck in the survey of writings on English teaching that Bethan presented to us that the comments tend to be teachers/proponents of the upper end of the spectrum who are defining what they think education is either in opposition to a reductive/materialist approach or, more positively, in terms that at least imply some sort of underlying image of the human being that sees us as more than a random collection of cells. The other end of the spectrum seems not to feel the need to justify their approach; this is something I will come back to later.

What is clear is a picture of these different positions battling for influence from the beginning. Thus Matthew Arnold starts by bemoaning our 'faith in machinery ... as if it had value in or for itself.'[3] The Newbolt Report in 1921 criticizes a view of English as 'merely acquaintance with a certain ... number of terms, or the power of spelling these terms correctly and arranging them without gross mistakes.'[4] Instead it posits a vision of English as connoting 'the discovery of the world by the first and most direct way open to us, and the discovery of ourselves in our native environment.' Newbolt continued with a characterization that has rarely been bettered by the 'top' of the spectrum, that 'the writing of English is essentially an art, and the effect of English Literature, in education, is the development of art upon the development of the human character.'

Peter Abbs asserted that F R Leavis in the Cambridge School 'gave powerful currency to the notion that the teacher, critic and artist had no choice but to oppose the destructive, seemingly inexorable drift of industrial civilization.'[5] Edmond Holmes devastatingly described the underlying attitudes in Western Education as requiring 'blind, passive, literal, unintelligent obedience'[6] adding that the child 'must become a tabula rasa before his teacher can write on it. The vital part of him, call it what you will, must become clay before his teacher can begin to mould him.'[7] In a terrifyingly close description of what my classmates in the MA were describing of their work, Holmes describes that the business of the teacher is 'to drill the child into the mechanical production of quasi-material results; and his success in doing this will be gauged in due course by an examination—a periodic test which is designed to measure, not the degree of growth which the child has made, but the industry of the teacher as indicated by the receptivity of the class.'[8] A more devastating critique of the situation we seem to find ourselves in I have not read.

The Wider Educational Debate

As discussed in Chapter One, this dichotomy in English reflects a wider dichotomy in education generally: that between what Ken Robinson calls, in Out of Our Minds, the Rationalist view of education and the Natural.

To briefly recap, the Traditional or Rationalist approach assumes that 'the powers of logic and deduction are the true hallmarks of independent thought; these powers are the most reliable source of knowledge of oneself and of the material world; true knowledge is objective and independent of cultural values and personal feelings.'[9] The assumption is that this kind of mind is developed through 'absorbing' bodies of knowledge generated by these logico-deductive powers and the main role of the teacher becomes 'to transmit bodies of knowledge.'[10]

The Natural educator has a different set of assumptions. In this view each child has 'innate talents and sensibilities.' Robinson outlines three major assumptions which underlie a Natural approach. I quote them here in full:

- Education should develop the whole child and not just their academic abilities. It should engage their feelings, physical development, moral education and creativity.
- Knowledge of the self is as important as knowledge of the external world. Exploring personal feelings and values is essential and so are opportunities to exercise imagination and self-expression.
- One of the main roles of teachers is to draw out the individual in every child. In this sense, education is a process of self-realization.[11]

This stream of thought Robinson sees as gaining educational impetus in the ideas of Rousseau encapsulated in *Emile*, published in 1780. Over the next two hundred years he says that many other pioneers of child-centred education developed their own systems. Among the names he mentions are two I will concentrate on, John Dewey (1859-1952) and Rudolf Steiner.

John Dewey: Education and Experience

Through a long and distinguished life, John Dewey worked, wrote and lectured tirelessly for what has become known as Progressive education. He developed new methods in the United States of America in his Laboratory school in which, Robinson says, 'teachers were encouraging learning by doing.' Experience is a word that he uses a great deal. In a late series of lectures given in 1938 and published as *Experience and Education*, Dewey analyses his ideas and the progressive movement in the light of the criticisms that both had received.

In these lectures Dewey identifies that the Progressive movement has suffered from a blind belief in 'departure from the old' which he says 'solves no problems.'[12] Even the belief that education comes about through experience is not safe, for experience can be 'miseducative.' There is the definite feeling that he is saying that it has been, on occasion, as miseducative in Progressive schools as Traditional ones.

The answer, says Dewey, is a coherent and carefully worked through 'philosophy of educative experience.'[13] This philosophy or 'conception of experience' must act as a frame for a plan for deciding on 'subject-matter, upon methods of instruction and discipline, and upon material equipment and social organization of the school.' Unless this is the case Dewey says that a school is 'wholly in the air.' He adds:

> Just because traditional education was a matter of routine in which plans and programs were handed down from the past, it does not follow that progressive education is a matter of planless improvisation.[14]

Dewey points out that traditional schools can get along 'without any consistently developed philosophy of education.' Adding bitterly that 'about all it required in that line was a set of abstract words like culture, discipline, our great cultural heritage, etc., actual guidance being derived not from them but from custom and established routines.'

How contemporary this sounds! I include two statements from Education Secretary Michael Gove which place him in Dewey's Traditional bracket. Here is one from a speech at the Conservative conference in Birmingham on 5 October 2010:

> We need to reform English—the great tradition of our literature—Dryden, Pope, Swift, Byron, Keats, Shelley, Austen, Dickens and Hardy—should be at the heart of our school life. Our literature is the best in the world—it is every child's birthright and we should be proud to teach it in every school.

Later, in a speech to Cambridge University on 24 November 2011, Gove elaborated:

> In an age before structuralism, relativism and post-modernism it seemed a natural and uncomplicated thing, the mark of civilisation, to want to spread knowledge, especially the knowledge of great human achievement, to every open mind.

It is as if Dewy in 1938 had actually met Michael Gove! In fact, he obviously had, inasmuch as Michael Gove is really, and I think pretty unconsciously, occupying an essentially Traditional paradigm. But, as Dewey explains, he does not feel the need to do more than cite abstract nouns because he feels that what stands behind them is self-explanatory. Dewey ends these lectures by explaining that Progressive education has had its problems but that this is because it is forging a new path and because of the 'failure' of its educators 'who professedly adopt [the standards, aims and methods of progressive education] to be faithful to them in practice.'[15] He continues:

> As I have emphasised more than once, the road of the new education is not an easier one to follow than the old road but a more strenuous and difficult one.

It will remain so until it has attained its majority and that attainment will require many years of serious co-operative work on the part of its adherents.

He ends with an impassioned plea:

> that the basic question concerns the nature of education with no qualifying adjectives prefixed. What we want and need is education pure and simple, and we shall make surer and faster progress when we devote ourselves to finding out just what education is and what conditions have to be satisfied in order that education may be a reality and not a name or a slogan. It is for this reason alone that I have emphasised the need for a sound philosophy of experience.[16]

I have quoted him extensively because, as a state-trained practitioner in an alternative and progressive educational movement, I experience everything he says here vividly. Now I would like to turn to someone who worked very hard to build a coherent philosophy of education.

Rudolf Steiner and *The Science of Knowing*: Outline of an Epistemology Implicit in the Goethean World View

At the tender age of 22, Rudolf Steiner was given the coveted job of editing Goethe's scientific works in a massive effort to collect together all his work, both artistic and scientific, in Weimar under Professors Kurshner and Schroer. Throughout the 1880s he worked through Goethe's papers, writing introductions to each part as it was published. As he did so he records in his 1924 preface of *Goethean Science* that:

> it seemed to me that nowhere in recent times were inner certainty, harmonious completeness, and a sense for reality with respect to the world as fully represented as in Goethe.[17]

In contrast he experienced the philosophical views of his time as tending to 'encapsulate itself within the being of man himself.'[18] He found that everywhere it was asserted that 'the human being, in his activity of knowing, strikes up against certain limits through which he cannot penetrate into the realm of true reality.'[19] Surely this is the crux of the matter: can the human being actually access 'true reality' or is s/he condemned to experience only a facsimile in the mode of Plato's Cave? Steiner made a study of the course that philosophy was taking in his time; tracing this dualism through Descartes and seeing it taken to its ultimate conclusion in Kant in his *Critique of Pure Reason* and his adherents. In *Goethean Science*, Steiner says that:

> Confronting all this there stood for me the fact—inwardly experienced, and known in the experiencing—that man with his thinking, if he deepens it sufficiently, does live in the midst of world reality as within a spiritual reality.[20]

Steiner adds that he 'believed that I possessed this knowledge as one that can stand in human consciousness with the same inner clarity as that which manifests in mathematical knowledge.'[21]

Steiner set out to develop an epistemology that reflected the methods of Goethe. As he says: 'It became clear to me how my thoughts led me to behold the essential being of knowledge that emerges everywhere in Goethe's creative activity and in his stance towards the world. I found that my viewpoints provided me with an epistemology that is the epistemology of the Goethean world view.'[22] He set this epistemology down in his *The Science of Knowing,* and in his books, *Goethe's World Conception* and *The Philosophy of Freedom,* both published in 1897. Writing in his preface of the 1924 edition of *The Science of Knowing,* Steiner comments that 'as I look at it again today, it also appears to me to be the epistemological foundation for everything I said and published later':[23] a remarkable claim of consistency over a period of nearly 40 years from the age of 26 until the year before his death at 64. Just as Goethe felt that although he was famous for his literature that his scientific work was his most important, Steiner asserted that his most important contribution to human development was the epistemology that he developed out of Goethe's work. It was out of this that all his later work and his educational movement came. He was utterly frustrated by the lack of understanding he met from his contemporaries. Even those who joined the Anthroposophical Society and tried to implement his ideas often failed to fully penetrate his epistemology. In October 1918, Steiner brought out his earlier books again saying that he felt that their message had been missed 21 years before.

Rudolf Steiner's Epistemology in *The Science of Knowing*

In a nutshell Steiner says that 'in the human being two regions confront each other; experience and thinking.'[24] I here summarize Steiner's view on both regions.

Experience

Moving through the world, objects in space and time approach us; we play no part in their coming about. To begin with, we can only let our gaze sweep across the manifoldness of objects confronting us. The activity that we do as human beings is to grasp these objects, reality, with our senses— only this can be called pure experience. Steiner says that it is not important that scientists think that the objects are only a product of an unknown molecular world; it is their colour, warmth and sounds etc. which lie before our thinking.[25]

With inner life this is not so clear; however, closer consideration shows that feelings appear on the horizon of our consciousness in the same way as the outer things. A feeling presses in on my consciousness in the same way that an impression of light does. Even thinking itself appears to us at first as an object of experience.

Experience then is 'mere juxtaposition in space and succession in time; an aggregate of utterly disconnected particulars.'[26] No object can be more or less important than any other, or we would have to bring thought and judgement to bear: they are a manifoldness of equal value.

If what we see as separate was all reality we could do nothing but describe what we see.[27] With mere experience, we can observe the objects but are unable to draw causal relations or connections between phenomena.

Thinking

The thing which can lead us out of this unconnectedness is thinking. 'Lawful interconnectedness' is present in thinking from its first appearance.

'Even as a fact of experience within experience, thinking occupies an exceptional position', Steiner continues in *The Science of Knowing*. 'With the rest of experience [other than thinking], I must penetrate the shell in order to arrive at the kernel; with thinking, shell and kernel are one undivided unity. *In thinking, what we must seek for with the rest of experience has itself become direct experience.*'[28]

'With this the solution is given which will hardly be solved in any other way. That we stick to experience is a justified demand of science. But no less so is the demand that we seek out the inner lawfulness of experience. *This inner being itself must therefore appear at someplace in experience as experience.*'[29]

'Only when we allow our thinking to work does reality first acquire true characterization. Reality, which before was mute, now speaks a clear language.

'*Our thinking is the translator that interprets for us the gestures of experience.*'[30]

This epistemology says that we *can* access reality through joining perception with thinking which creates what Steiner calls the act of knowledge.[31] He maintains that the fact that 'reality has separated itself into two realms, perception and thinking' leads us to feel that they are separate. This, he says, is an illusion created by our self-conscious separation from the world. In the activity of knowing we reunite what has been separated by our intellect.

In *Thinking Beyond the Brain,* Marilyn Schlitz sets out three 'important metaphysical assumptions that limit the ability of science to integrate alternative viewpoints'. These assumptions seem to me to apply to Education as well. Here they are:

> a. *Realism* (ontological-leads to epistemological conclusion). There is a real material world independent of mind which is, in essence, physically measurable (positivism). We are embedded in that world, follow its laws, and have evolved from an ancient origin. Mind or consciousness evolved within that world; the world pre-existed before its appearance, and continues to exist and persist independent of consciousness.
>
> b. *Objectivism* (epistemological and ontological) a form of materialist realism which says that the world is knowable and persists as a domain of objects unaffected by perceiving subjects. That real world therefore can be studied as object. That is, it is accessible to sense perception and can be consensually observed and validated.
>
> c. *Reductionism* (epistemological) knowledge is attained by a process of analysing, explaining, or validating data in terms of the constituent parts of objects and/or the laws which determine their behaviour. The real world is described by the laws of physics, which are believed to apply everywhere. The essence of the scientific endeavour is to provide explanations for complex phenomena in terms of the characteristics of, and interaction among, their component parts.[32]

These assumptions underlie our thinking. The ontological experience of the split between our outer and inner world leads us to assume the above as our unconscious epistemology. Through all the ages spiritual leaders have emphasized that this is an illusion. Studies of 'flow' and optimal experience show a close correlation with mystical experience.[33]

If Steiner is right and thinking does connect us to reality, how do we access that?

It seems that when experiences of flow occur that the person experiencing flow experiences the subject/object dissolve. At that moment the illusion of separation is overcome and the ontological experience coincides with Steiner's epistemology.

Is this proof that Steiner's epistemology is right? I think so; though I also think that within the confines of this chapter I cannot say enough to prove it to you. You would have to go to the source and read the book for yourself (that is what nobody seems to do—even most Anthroposophists!). It seems to me that it is this epistemology of the reality of thinking and of its relationship to experience that would save us from the 'grey pall of assessment' that seems to be spreading around the globe.

Intellect and Reason

Steiner says that we have two kinds of thinking. Intellect (*Verstand*) he characterizes as creating sharply delineated concepts, he then says that reason brings the individual concepts into a unified whole. The first is an activity that makes distinctions; the second is an activity that joins. He says that the first is much more prevalent in the sciences, and in fact a lot of people think that this is all there is in thinking. Steiner says that this is a 'necessary preliminary stage of any higher scientific work.'[34]

Reason (*Vernunft*) allows the concepts created by the intellect to pass over into one another. Steiner continues:

> If I bring a number of single thoughts into living flux in such a way that they pass over into one another, connect with one another, then thought configurations arise that are present only for reason, that the intellect cannot attain. For reason, the creations of the intellect give up their separate existences and live on only as part of the totality.[35]

This, Steiner is convinced, is an activity which overcomes the object/subject divide:

> reason is the ability to bring harmony to light when harmony lies within the object itself … reason brings into view the higher unity of the intellect's concepts, a unity that the intellect certainly has in its configurations but is unable to see.[36]

Steiner based all his work on his epistemology and his educational ideas derive directly from there. Embedded in his pedagogy is the striving to 'remove obstacles' in the child's development and to strengthen their capacity not only for intellectual work but to experience reason.

Jerome Bruner and Two Modes of Thinking

In Chapter 1 *Approaching the Literary*, Bruner asks the question: 'What makes great stories reverberate with such liveliness in our ordinarily mundane minds? What gives great fiction its power: what in the text and what in the reader?'[37] Though a difficult question, he feels that the task is both possible and worthwhile because it 'might shed light not only on literary issues but on psychological ones beyond the limits of the psychology of literature.'[38]

So, in Chapter 2, Jerome Bruner states his argument:

> There are two modes of cognitive functioning, two modes of thought, each providing distinctive ways of ordering experience, of constructing reality.[39]

He characterizes them as:

> The paradigmatic or logico-scientific one attempts to fulfil the ideal of a
> formal, mathematical system of description and explanation. It employs
> categorisation or conceptualisation and the operations by which categories
> are established, instantiated, idealised, and related one to the other to form
> a system.[40]

He says that we know a great deal about this kind of thinking and have
developed logic, mathematics, sciences and automata for operating in these
fields. He says that, on the whole we have developed ways to help students
operate in the paradigmatic mode. He adds 'the imaginative application of
the paradigmatic mode leads to good theory, tight analysis, logical proof,
sound argument, and empirical discovery guided by reasoned hypothesis'
and he adds that 'there is a heartlessness to logic.'[41]

By contrast the narrative mode leads to:

> good stories, gripping drama, believable (though not necessarily 'true') his-
> torical accounts. It deals in human or human-like intention and action and
> the vicissitudes and consequences that mark their course. It strives to put its
> timeless miracles into the particulars of experience in time and place.[42]

Bruner adds that we 'know precious little in any formal sense' about how
narrative mode works. Perhaps, he posits, this is because it must construct
'two landscapes simultaneously,' one of action the 'story grammar' and one
of the 'psychic reality' of the characters. He continues that it is the narrative
mode that he wants to investigate, and that in the form of its 'farthest
reach'; as an art form. As he says, to understand the paradigmatic mode we
might study the works of the great mathematicians, so to understand the
narrative, we must study the work of great and trained writers.

Bruner begins by stating that narrative deals with the 'vicissitudes
of human intentions.' He contrasts this with the law of cause and effect
that is fundamental to the paradigmatic mode. He cites an experiment
by Fritz Heider and Marianne Simmel in which a 'bare' animated
film demonstrated the 'irresistibility of perceived intention.' In it they
created a scenario involving a small moving triangle, a small moving
circle, a large moving square, and a box-like empty rectangle. Their
movements were 'irresistibly seen as two lovers being pursued by a large
bully who, upon being thwarted, broke up the house in which he tried to
find them.'[43] So, Bruner concludes that intention is primary in narrative
and that we plainly see 'search', 'goal-seeking', 'persistence in overcoming obstacles' and we see them as intention driven.

I experienced the power of this at the 2013 Edinburgh Festival. A children's performance became one of the hits. It involved watching a man
sellotape a carrier bag together so that it had a rudimentary head and

arms and then make it 'dance' within a circle of large fans. Almost every movement seemed expressive and as more carrier bags were added the story became more and more complex. Adults and children alike were spellbound by their own narratives constructed spontaneously from the circling movements of plastic bags. It was striking how inwardly active one was, selecting the movements which suited the narrative.

Connections with Rudolf Steiner's *The Science of Knowing*

I am struck by the connections between Bruner's ideas expressed in 1986 and Steiner's written exactly one hundred years before. Steiner also identifies a paradigmatic mode of thought which he characterizes as having a categorizing function (*Verstand*) and a form in which this kind of thinking employs reason (*Vernunft*) to relate the categories together to form a system. Steiner says that this kind of thinking is appropriate to understand the inorganic world which operates according to the law of cause and effect.

To understand the organic world, however, we need a different kind of thinking. One which can penetrate to what Goethe called the typus, or biological archetype. In literature, it seems to me that there is a correlation between the typus and genre; a matter that I explored in my first chapter, 'Riding the Magic Carpet.'

In the humanities, on the other hand, Steiner says that we must concentrate on the idea as it manifests in the individual human being: 'whereas in organic science the general, the idea of the typus, must always be kept in view, in the humanities the idea of the personality must be maintained.'[44] Steiner emphasizes the agency of the idea or intention, coming from within as the significant study in the humanities. This corresponds to Bruner's observation that literature operates through a study of the 'vicissitudes of intention.'

In reading Bruner, Pope, Steiner and others, the picture has been building in me that literature works through recreation. The writer encapsulates their experience in words. The reader reads the words. There is a mystery in the way that they resurrect the meaning laid down there. It is a process of 'reading between the lines', of picking up implications. It seems to be related to genre in that there are forms which they are using as a sort of template. Each reading is an act of creation by an individual. What the writer lays down is a code that contains possible worlds. What the reader creates is a new world that becomes part of an emerging cultural reality. Perhaps this is why it often feels that it is English and English Literature study that stand at the vanguard of a push back against the murky flood of reductionist assessment.

Steiner asserts that;

> Reason leads back to reality again. The unity of all existence, which before was *felt* or of which one even had only dim inklings, is clearly penetrated and seen by reason. The intellectual view must be deepened by the view of reason. If the former is regarded as an end in itself instead of as a necessary intermediary stage, then it does not yield reality but rather a distorted image of it.[45]

This is, for me, the crux of the matter. In all the books on creativity that I have read there seems to be an implicitly emerging sense that the human being is participating in her/his own emergence. For this to be valid, the human being must be able to access reality. I believe that Rudolf Steiner has succeeded in forging an epistemology that confirms the Romantic worldview of Goethe. It is upon this epistemology of creative inner activity that he has founded his educational movement, and that I believe can guide us in forging a new path of a truly progressive education which allows the flowering of each human to their full potential. In the next chapter, I explore the moment of insight experienced when this creative inner activity is encouraged within a lesson.

Chapter Three

THE ACT OF KNOWING
AND THE A-HA MOMENT IN THE CLASSROOM

[In which Liz describes a class taking off into consistently free thinking; describes the components, characteristics and history of 'a-ha' moments; she investigates how to create the conditions for a-ha moments through constructivist teaching methods; and how to create a rigorous, context-rich and child-centred education with a conscious epistemological underpinning. She goes on to cover Robinson's discussion of sciences' view of the material and inner world as separate in contrast to the Romantics' more interconnected worldview; recaps Goethe's four steps and dives into Steiner's epistemology, which she contends is a radical assertion of the possibility for the human being to contact reality through thinking; she finishes by exploring the potential of formative assessment as a useful template for active learning techniques.]

The A-ha Moment

When was the last time that you had an a-ha moment? Have you had one in the last week? Do you ever remember having one at school? How do you feel when you do have one?

One of my proudest moments in teaching was in the summer of 2013, when I asked my AS group to review the year we had just had and one student said; 'We had so many a-ha moments!' For me, these moments are the essence of success as a teacher.

In the summer of 2012, I had just finished my most fulfilling year of teaching to date. I sat down to try to record why. This is a sample of what I wrote:

> In the course of this academic year I have experienced fulfilling teaching of an order I have not known before. This is an attempt to understand how and why.
>
> With a group of eight 17-18 year olds I studied literature. We started with literary theory including Marxism, feminism, metaphor and ideas of literary value, much referenced ideas from structuralist and post-structuralist thinkers. We applied these ideas to texts of the students' choice. Then we took *Wuthering Heights* and they chose a novel with which to compare it. They enjoyed this process, finding it stimulating.

In the spring term we began the study of the Gothic genre, beginning with *Paradise Lost*. Instantly the group took off! Somehow this topic and this text, building on the foundations we had established, allowed their thinking to become free in a consistent way that was breathtaking for all of us. We found ourselves looking at each other with (in Keats' words) 'a wild surmise'; in the same state of inspired excitement as I described in the *Midsummer Night's Dream* lesson in Chapter One.

Everyone was free and not all of us were doing it all the time. However, collectively and over time, we were helping each other to develop our thinking. We were literally thinking 'outside the box' in ways that felt inspired. It felt as if we had created a sort of chalice around the classroom table. There we experienced communion and community.

The students themselves were, at their own levels, aware that something magical was happening and expressed it both at the time and at their graduation; talking about 'the remarkable development of concepts', 'independent' and 'expanded thinking' but also acknowledging that they could not adequately describe what they had experienced. This is the essence of a learning community and I had experienced it before through English, both myself, and in observing my colleague Josie Alwyn. It seems to me that this year reached higher, more consistently and with less input from me than previously.

Why? I think that the concepts which lie behind the A-level specification have been helpful in releasing an energy inherent in the study of literature as art.

As you can see these notes are full of wonder and speculation as to how this could have happened. Writing these notes was the beginning of a quest that I am still on. That group are long gone but the experience has continued and deepened, though each group is different.

I have already written about the extraordinary lesson that I experienced with my new AS class with *A Midsummer Night's Dream*. In this lesson a student (H) had an a-ha moment that set off a whole new level of thinking in the group. This gave me an abiding interest in these epiphany moments.

Characteristics of an Epiphany Moment

I have a clear memory of an a-ha moment in my own education. I was seven and our teacher was telling us about the water cycle. She explained how water evaporates from the ocean to form clouds and she asked us how we thought the water got back to the ocean again. In contemplating this I 'saw' the whole cycle conceptually and shot up my hand. I vividly remember the excitement of 'seeing' this cycle and my certainty it was correct. The smile of recognition that I received from the teacher warms my soul close to half a century later (I was not a particularly precocious scholar). I remember very little of my education, and most of the memories I do have are more to do with difficulties, but this one is vivid and suffused with positive joy and energy.

More research into these moments would be fascinating. This one, it seems to me, has several classic components. The teacher had introduced several related phenomena, but had held back the overarching concept. The question elicited inner activity in me in which I combined the information, brought it together with my experience of rain and rivers, and 'saw' a, for me, new pattern that made sense of a vital part of my world. I saw this pattern instantly and whole, and I intuitively felt that what I was perceiving was correct. Connected to this was a surge of joy and a feeling of self-competency. The experience is associated with a remarkably strong recall of the event in which I can remember where I was sitting, where the teacher was standing, and the connected emotions.

I have begun to recognize the physical characteristics of these moments. They usually follow periods of intense engagement in studying the text; sometimes for weeks. Then suddenly a pupil will become very animated, they will often start to shake with excitement. Their eyes widen, and their gaze is often unfocused—it is as if they are seeing both forwards and backwards at once. There is a huge intake of breath followed by an exclamation of the perception that they are having. This can sometimes be quite incoherent at first, as they try to express something that they have understood but which is stretching their capacity to express it. Often the group can help by grasping the perception whole and actually analysing it into its constituent parts. The group also becomes animated as they tune into the new levels of understanding that are being generated. The pace of learning increases exponentially.

This seems to me the Holy Grail of Literature Teaching, and all other teaching too!

History

The most famous example of an a-ha moment is from Ancient Greece and is thought to be a myth: Archimedes is said to have worked out the way to measure the volume of an irregular object whilst having a bath and to have run down the street shouting 'Eureka!' (I have found it) thus giving this experience its name. The a-ha moment is first recorded in the Oxford English Dictionary as a formal term for this in 1939.

It is also known as 'insight' or 'epiphany' in psychological terms. Insight is used to describe the process in problem solving when a previously unsolvable puzzle becomes suddenly clear. This is often accompanied by an exclamation of joy or satisfaction: it is significant that both Eureka! and A-ha! are followed by exclamation marks to express this!

In *Gaining Insight into the 'Aha'-experience*, Topolinski and Reber described four defining attributes:

1. The a-ha moment appears suddenly.
2. The solution to the problem can be processed smoothly, or fluently.
3. It elicits positive affect.
4. A person experiencing the a-ha moment is convinced that the solution is true.[1]

A fifth aspect which was researched in *Effort toward Comprehension: Elaboration or 'Aha'?* is that while elaboration had no positive effect on recall, a-ha moments were associated with better recall.[2] Interestingly, the Eureka effect on memory was only found to occur when there was initial confusion. Subjects were given confusing sentences to consider and after a while a 'clue' word that helped them make sense of it. If the clue word was given first there was no increased effect on memory. This points to the importance of the student's *active* involvement.

Creating the Conditions

So how does a teacher create the conditions for this? In Chapter One, 'Riding the Magic Carpet', I investigated the question of how this special lesson took off. There I came to the conclusion that it was connected to a structuralist approach to literature that corresponded to a Goethean approach to literature, to an active learning style and the fostering of a strong ethos of a learning community. Since then I have also felt that it is connected to the actual nature of the a-ha moment and that this may be related to the 'act of knowing' as described by Steiner in *The Philosophy of Freedom* and to the constructivist techniques[3] that I use in my classroom. If we can find a rigorous method for delivering learning that puts the activity of the student at the centre we will truly have accessed the holy grail of teaching. Then, maybe, Education Secretary Michael Gove will appreciate progressive methods! However, at the moment things seem to be moving in the other direction.

The Problem: Filling Buckets or Lighting Fires?

On Saturday 22 March 2014, *The Times* newspaper ran a story about the head of Ofsted Sir Michael Wilshaw. It was entitled 'Lives were ruined by child-led learning, says Ofsted chief.' In the first sentence Sir Michael was quoted as saying that 'he would personally root out any inspectors who defied his orders and promoted progressive teaching methods.' Apparently he went further after his speech saying that his position was based on personal experience:

I am part of a generation of people who experienced—I started teaching in the 1960s—that sort of ideology, which ruined the lives of generations of children at that time.

Progressive teaching methods are not in vogue at Ofsted then!

In my first MA module *Performance Arts in the Classroom* we had a plethora of ex-teachers now working in the Arts who came to talk to us about their initiatives. All were passionate about creativity and child-centred learning; but all were also keen to assure us that their initiatives were *rigorous*, that they were not the sort of laissez-faire style of the 1960s where no check was kept on the learning and progress of the pupils.

In Steiner schools, we have a very coherent vision of child development and have worked up a coherent curriculum; but I have sometimes felt that our techniques lag behind. I have always been grateful for my state training at Newcastle in the 1980s in which I was lucky enough to be trained by some of the most creative teacher trainers of the time in Don Kent for English and Dorothy Heathcote for Drama in Education. There I was introduced to an ethos of mixed-ability group work in English and drawing on the child's powers of imagination in Drama.

Problems of technique in Steiner education are particularly acute in Upper Schools (aged 14-18) because Steiner did not live long enough to give very comprehensive ideas about the ways in which this age-group should be taught. This leaves teachers, often undertrained, falling back on their own experiences of education. I remember commenting to my colleague when I started working at the Edinburgh Steiner School that I felt I was just delivering a 'soft' version of mainstream teaching not really something radically new. I felt that I had not penetrated the way that I could maximize learning for my students. So I know what Sir Michael Wilshaw is talking about and it *is* important.

Does that mean, however, that we must abandon child-centred learning in favour of the 'filling buckets' approach that Michael Gove and his inspectorate seem to favour? I do not believe it does. There is too much evidence that creative, context rich, and imaginative learning works. But it is a challenge to us to become much more conscious of the epistemological basis on which we operate.

Living in Two Worlds

In his book *Out of Our Minds*, Ken Robinson explains that one of the founding perceptions of modern philosophy is that 'we live in two distinct worlds'; the material, objective world, and our own inner, subjective world of sensations, thoughts and feelings.[4] He states that this raises fundamental questions for the modern person; 'How do we come to see the external world as we do? How do we know that it's really there and not just in our minds? How do we get *out of our minds*?.'[5] The last question forms the title of the book.

Robinson points out that for everyday purposes we assume that the material, objective world is there and this has been called the 'natural attitude', or I prefer naïve realism. He argues that science has been busily setting about 'bringing it under our control.'[6] This has resulted in a view of the world 'out there' about which we have to inform ourselves. This stands against another view, championed by Romanticism that there is a vital connection between our inner world and the outer one. This has largely been upheld by artists and tends to be disregarded by the naïve realists and scientists as subjective.

Two Traditions

As discussed in the previous chapters, Ken Robinson identifies that these two world views lead to two kinds of educator; the 'Rational Individualist' and the 'Natural Individualist.'[7] Rational individualism sees knowledge as information and is recognizable in the pronouncements of Education Secretary Michael Gove and Ofsted Chief Inspector Sir Michael Wilshaw.

Natural individualism makes completely different assumptions according to Robinson. Above all, he argues that 'naturalists want to address the whole child: mind, body and spirit.'[8] Naturalist attitudes gained ground in the 1950s and 1960s, says Robinson, 'partly because they were seen as representing a more egalitarian approach to education' and that Naturalists argued that 'academic education marginalised feelings, intuition, aesthetic sensibilities and creativity—the very qualities that make human beings human.'[9]

Robinson sees problems with both in that he feels both 'reinforce the division between intellect and emotion.' The Rationalists emphasize the intellect over the feeling life. He sees natural individualism as a reaction against '*objectivism*; against treating knowledge as impersonal.' He identifies a danger that natural individualism moves too far the other way towards '*subjectivism*: to thinking of individual consciousness as completely independent from the world of others.'[10] It is this problem that I think Sir Michael Wilshaw is reacting against in *The Times*.

Robinson continues by contrasting scientific and artistic ways of approaching the world and calling for a synthesis of these in a 'New Renaissance.'[11] He clearly sees Science as having an 'objectivism' bias and Art as having a 'subjectivism' one. He does not, however, as far as I am aware, propose a new epistemology. In my last chapter, 'Two Modes of Thinking', I identified that one of the reasons that the Rationalist mindset seems to have the upper hand, on the whole, is because of what I feel is the 'epistemological gap' at the foundations of education. This allows Michael Gove and even educationalists such as Sir Michael Wilshaw to return to the default position of a naïve realist when worries about standards raise their head. It means that teachers can, through a lack of confidence, ignore years of research that show that richly imaginative contexts in education enhance learning.

The Naturalist Stream

In this chapter, I will further explore the two people who have bridged this divide; Johan Wolfgang von Goethe and Rudolf Steiner. Goethe through applying his highly developed artistic sensibilities to the study of science, and Rudolf Steiner by taking Goethe's synthesis of artistic sensibility and scientific exactitude and applying it to thinking, to the way human beings make sense of the world, and thereby forging a new epistemology.

In my previous chapter 'Riding the Magic Carpet', I demonstrated how I felt that following Goethe's scientific approach to literature exponentially enhanced learning in my classroom. In 'Two Modes of Thinking', I argued that Steiner's epistemology, developed from Goethe's scientific approach, could be seen as a way of defending education from a materialist/reductive/rationalist approach to learning. Here I would like to show the relationship between Goethe's worldview, Steiner's epistemology, and the active-learning techniques of the constructivist classroom. This is a synthesis that would seem to me to bridge the abyss that Robinson has identified between objectivism and subjectivism, and explain the a-ha moment.

Goethe's Scientific Method

In his edition of Goethe's *The Metamorphosis of Plants*, Gordon L. Miller says that Goethe 'envisioned a fuller integration of poetic and scientific sensibilities that would provide a way of experiencing nature both symbolically and scientifically simultaneously.'[12] Miller adds that it is his belief that 'Goethe's way of science offers hope for lessening the modern alienation from nature that not only diminishes the beauty and joy of human life but also fuels environmental irresponsibility and apathy.'[13] These lofty ideals may sound a long way from the travails of the classroom, but this chapter is an attempt to draw them together!

Goethe identified four steps in his scientific method, which I will recap again briefly. The first stage is rigorous observation of the phenomena, whilst holding preformed concepts back. In my literature teaching this takes the form of a lively experience of the text without any conceptual input from me as the teacher; I just act to facilitate the activities.

The second stage is 'exact sensory perception.' The discrete phenomena are brought into movement or connection. In plant study Goethe thought the plant's development through time; both backwards and forwards. In my literature teaching this corresponds with arriving at an overview of the text through designing activities that facilitate students' active engagement with the structural relationships (motifs, scenes, verses, chapters etc.).

The third stage is where the participant experiences, in Goethe's words, 'the dynamic inward archetype' or the 'Urphenomenon.' Goethe claimed that he could perceive the archetypal plant. This is the stage at which my students described their experience in 'Riding the Magic Carpet' with *A Midsummer Night's Dream* thus: 'the whole play suddenly opened up/unfolded and showed us all its secrets/meanings' (M); 'the whole play opened up, exposing layers, it revealed itself and we made the links' (J).

Miller explains that 'what was successive in one's empirical experience then becomes simultaneous in the intuitively perceived idea—*Proteus in potentia*. Instead of an onlooking subject knowing an alien object, this is knowledge through participation, or even identification, of observer and observed—knowing things from the inside'. This is the shift from intellect to what Goethe called Reason which I investigated in the chapter 'Two Modes of Thinking.' It is also intimately related to the a-ha moment.

The fourth stage is an engagement of the will through the overcoming of the subject/object divide. For my students in 'Riding the Magic Carpet' this took the form, even in the most avowedly lazy ones, of wanting to sit down and write their AS coursework essays there and then!

Rudolf Steiner became the foremost expert on Goethe's scientific work through being his scientific editor for the Weimar Archives in the 1880s. He took Goethe's method one step further by turning it on the activity of thinking itself; an act of meta-cognition through which he arrived at a new epistemology.

The Act of Knowing

In the chapter 'Two Modes of Thinking', I concentrated on the book which Rudolf Steiner published in 1886 entitled *The Science of Knowing: an Epistemology*, based on *Goethe's World View* which, 40 years later, he averred 'contained all my subsequent work in germinal form.'[14] In 1888 Steiner met the philosopher Eduard von Hartmann, a pessimist. His translator, Michael Wilson, says that in his papers he describes the 'chilling effect on him of the way this philosopher of pessimism denied that thinking could ever reach reality, but must forever deal with illusions.' He had already established his epistemology; however, in 1894 he brought out a book called *The Philosophy of Freedom* in which he deals more explicitly with the views of philosophers such as Hartmann and Bishop Berkeley. In this book, written consciously to counter the rationalism that Robinson identifies as separating us from our feelings, Steiner addresses the way that thinking can reconnect us to the world. His book therefore addresses the concerns of this chapter most directly. Whilst *The Science of Knowing* described Steiner's position in germinal form he felt that *The Philosophy of Freedom* described the foundations on which his subsequent work stood, including his educational approach. In it the act of knowledge is portrayed vigorously and rigorously as an *activity*, and it is that activity which I want to concentrate on here.

Right from the beginning Steiner wants us to be aware that he is tackling *the* fundamental issues of human existence and that his treatment is *active* as befits his method. In the preface to *The Philosophy of Freedom*, he elucidates the two fundamental questions which he seeks to address:

1. Is it possible to find a view of the essential nature of man such as will give us a foundation for everything else that comes to meet us—whether through life experience or through science—which we feel is otherwise not self-supporting and therefore liable to be driven by doubt and criticism into the realm of uncertainty?
2. Is man entitled to claim for himself freedom of will, or is freedom a mere illusion begotten of his inability to recognize the threads of necessity on which his will, like any natural event, depends?

He continues:

> This book is intended to show that the experiences which the second problem causes man's soul to undergo depend upon the position he is able to take up towards the first problem. An attempt is made to prove that there is a view of the nature of man's being which can support the rest of knowledge; and further, that this view completely justifies the idea of free will, provided only that we have first discovered that region of the soul in which free will can unfold itself.[15]

So this book will really attempt to meet the most fundamental questions in order to establish a firm foundation for an epistemology.

Now for the method: Steiner says that the answers given will not be of the 'purely theoretical sort which, once mastered, may be carried about as a conviction preserved by memory.' This would, he says, be no real answer at all for the manner of thinking on which the book is based. The book will instead 'point to a field of experience in which man's inner *soul activity* supplies a living answer to these questions at every moment that he needs one.'[16]

Steiner adds that 'in this book the aim is a philosophical one—that knowledge itself shall come organically alive.' This way of describing philosophy and knowledge feels very ahead of its time in 1886 and is more reminiscent of the post-modernist, post-structuralist and deconstructionist writing of Felix Guattari, Michel Foucault, Jacques Derrida or Julia Kristeva.

In *The Philosophy of Freedom,* Chapter 6 'The Act of Knowing,' Steiner establishes that in order to make sense of the world we have to think. We use thinking to make sense of our primary perceptions which would only be a meaningless series of events if we did not bring thinking to bear on them. Thinking, he says, is the only percept* we have which is produced by ourselves. Therefore it is transparent to our gaze. We can see it coming into being and, with self-discipline, we can direct it. This is the starting point for freedom; when we can know that our thinking is a free deed.

Here is an exercise which can demonstrate this. Take an ordinary object, a button or a mug and think three very clear and observational thoughts about it. You created these thoughts as a free deed; you were not affected by emotions or self-interest. Initially it is a small area of freedom, but it has massive implications.

He explains that the naïve realist thinks that their thinking in is their head and 'has nothing to do with the things' that they are thinking about.[17] He vigorously questions that with:

> What right have you to declare the world to be complete without thinking? Does not the world produce thinking in the heads of men with the same necessity as it produces the blossom on a plant? Plant a seed in the earth. It puts forth root and stem, it unfold into leaves and blossoms. Set the plant before yourself. It connects itself, in your mind, with a definite concept. Why should this concept belong any less to the whole plant than a leaf and blossom? You say the leaves and the blossom exist quite apart from a perceiving subject, but the concept appears only when a human being confronts the plant. Quite so. But leaves and blossoms also appear on the plant only if there is soil in which the seed can be planted, and light and air in which the leaves and blossom can unfold. Just so the concept of a plant arises when a thinking consciousness approaches the plant.[18]

This is a radical assertion of the possibility for the human being to contact reality through thinking. An education that really took this into consideration would find ways for students to access this experience both

---

* For an understanding of Liz's use of percept and concept, see 'Notes on the Translation': *The Philosophy of Freedom*. Steiner, R. Trans. Michael Wilson. (Rudolf Steiner Press, London, 2011) p. xix.

in Arts and Sciences. Progressive educators have always felt that there is something intrinsically within the human being that it is their job to 'draw out' (the meaning of *'educare'* in Latin). In Goethe's science we have a method, and in Steiner's epistemology we have a bridge, through which the human being connects subjectivism and objectivism. An education that could base itself on knowing as an activity in which percept and concept are dynamically connected through the agency of the child would truly draw on the primary source of human creativity.

A Dynamic Analogy

I have an analogical example which I had as an a-ha moment two years ago during a demonstration on light and complementary colours and which gives me a way to understand the dynamic of a conception of the world that dawns from within.

Take a small patch of any colour (bright ones work best, and bright yellow most clearly) and train your eyes on it unwaveringly for one minute. Then move your gaze to the side. There you will see a gently luminous colour. If it was yellow you will see violet (blue and red mixed); blue and you will see orange (red and yellow mixed); look at red and you will see green (blue and yellow mixed). The eye produces what is called the 'complementary' colour which is made up of the missing wavelengths in the colour we are looking at. This is analogical to the activity of paying attention to the phenomena as percepts and allowing the corresponding concepts to arise from within as a 'dawning realization.'

That Goethe knew this is explained by Alan P. Cottrell, a Goethean scientist, in his essay 'The Resurrection of Thinking; Goethe's New Scientific Attitude.'[19] He quotes Goethe describing this phenomenon and finishing with the sentence: 'a single colour calls forth within the eye by means of a specific sensation the striving for universality.'[20] Cottrell explains:

> It should now be clear that the activity of the eye, for Goethe, is vividly analogous to that of the mind itself...the eye of the body is stimulated by light and colour and responds actively by its very nature... the eye of the mind is stimulated by observations and thoughts, and responds through the intentional activity of *thinking*. The activity that occurs in *perception* on a rudimentary level of consciousness is raised by the mind to the fully conscious clarity of thinking. And from there it passes over to the even more intensely conscious activity of the observation of thinking itself.'[21]

Surely the a-ha moment is related to this experience. Cottrell continues:

> The facile distinction between 'objective' and 'subjective' knowledge is thus overcome through the new participatory mode of cognition, which is

Goethe's legacy to modern science, and which answers in a responsible and healthy way the age-old call: 'Know thyself.'[22]

We move from a view of the world that is separated and from which we are separate—secondary consciousness—to an understanding of ourselves and the world as a unity—participatory consciousness.

The Relationship to Mainstream Technique

It may be very interesting, even essential, to know this and I argued in the last chapter 'Two Modes of Thinking' that a knowledge of this would act as a defence against reductionist approaches to education, but how does it translate into practice?

Goethe's approach is also known as Phenomenology. It asks its adherents to:

1. Observe exactly, without bringing preconceptions to the observations.
2. Bring the phenomenon into active relationship to each other.
3. Listen inwardly to perceive 'dawning realizations.'
4. Act on intuitions.

One educator who has written about this is Geoff Petty. Whilst some of his premises seem lacking in in-depth research, his ideas in *Teaching Today* and *Evidence-Based Teaching*[23] show a close relationship to Goethe's phenomenology. His idea that we think in a language-free 'mentalese', which we need to translate into conscious thinking in order to construct meaning for ourselves, leads him to advocate a very active learning style and to endorse constructivist approaches. Approaches such as 'the flipped classroom' and Socratic questioning are helpful here.

These correspond to the educational approaches used in 'The Constructivist Classroom' as described by Shirley Clarke in *Formative Assessment in the Secondary Classroom*. Her list of twelve attributes of the constructivist classroom are culled from Brooks and Brooks (2003). As she says, 'the characteristics of the constructivist classroom inevitably include the use of *formative assessment.*'[24] I include them here, complete with her additional comments, and with my connections to Goethean science where appropriate, as the most concise list I know that shows an active approach (Clarke's additions are in italics as in the text—mine are in brackets).

1. Constructivist teachers encourage and accept student autonomy and initiative—*students frame their own questions and find answers* (students are inwardly active through questioning).
2. Constructivist teachers use raw data and primary sources, along with manipulative, interactive and physical materials—*students*

look for evidence rather than receiving knowledge passively and link concepts to real-life situations, events and objects (students employ exact observation of phenomena).

3. When framing tasks, constructivist teachers use cognitive terminology such as 'classify', 'analyse', 'predict' and 'create'—*teachers go beyond literal questions of how, what and who, thus encouraging high-level thinking* (tasks require students to bring their observations into movement in order to facilitate their own, new perceptions).

4. Constructivist teachers allow student responses to drive lessons, shift instructional strategies and alter content—*the curriculum and exam syllabi determine what must be taught, not how...whether the learning objective is being met or not is the prime concern-lesson content should change to best facilitate student learning* (child-centred learning).

5. Constructivist teachers inquire about students' understandings of concepts before sharing their own understanding of these concepts—*concept mapping or brainstorming before unit planning takes place, or at the beginnings of lessons, ensures that the teacher takes account of students' current understandings and interests* (student engagement is central and planned for).

6. Constructivist teachers encourage students to engage in dialogue, both with the teacher and with one another—*students are encouraged to present their own ideas as well as being permitted to hear and reflect on the ideas of others; paired two-minute discussions before general feedback leads to more powerful construction of new understandings or reflections of old ones* (active engagement is paramount).

7. Constructivist teachers encourage student enquiry by asking thoughtful, open-ended questions and encouraging students to ask questions of each other—*teachers use a range of questioning strategies to ensure maximum involvement, thinking and articulation* (it is the inner connection to a question which calls the inner 'sunrise', or 'dawning realization' to arise).

8. Constructivist teachers seek elaboration of students' initial responses—*by using a multiple-choice approach: 'What exactly do you mean? Do you mean this..., do you mean that..., or do you have an idea of your own?'* (encouraging honing of the conception).

9. Constructivist teachers engage students in experiences that might engender contradictions to their initial hypotheses and then encourage discussion—*teachers ask questions which set up contradictions to encourage discussion: e.g. 'So it is wrong to steal. But would it still be wrong to rob a bank if your children were starving?'* (further engaging students in defending/reconstructing their concepts actively).

10. Constructivist teachers allow 'wait time' after posing questions—*students need approximately five seconds after the question is asked—experimenting with 'no hands up' and talking partners, so all have a chance of being asked and the negative comparison effect is avoided* (more chance for the a-ha moment).

11. Constructivist teachers provide time for students to construct relationships and create metaphors—*asking 'what if?' questions to encourage links between ideas and giving students time to create metaphors for their understandings* (again bringing perceptions into movement, therefore more chance for an a-ha moment)

12. Constructivist teachers nurture students' natural curiosity through frequent use of the learning cycle model—*(1) students interact with selected materials and generate questions and hypotheses; (2) teacher focuses student's questions as a way of introducing the concept; (3) students work on new problems as a way of applying the concept* (active learning techniques build on each other for enhanced progress).

I would argue, these steps are a useful template for Active Learning techniques which would create the best conditions for the a-ha moment. The second part of this book, 'Cultivating the Conditions for A-ha Moments and Living Thinking in the Classroom', offers a practical guide.

During an a-ha moment, the student seems to me to resemble, figuratively, a Janus figure (the Roman god January, the turn of the year) with one face turned towards the phenomena and the other to the inner world of the concept; acting as an interface between the two.[*] The release of joy that we feel when we make a sure connection between the two is analogous to the meeting of matter and anti-matter and the release of energy engendered there. If we could help to create a world in which people could access that joy as a *modus vivendi* we could genuinely say, with Miranda in Shakespeare's *The Tempest*:

'Oh, brave new world that hath such people in't!'

---

[*] A further explanation of the human being looking into the past and future, the phenomena and the concept, can be found in the footnote on p. 61.

Chapter Four

CREATING THE CONDITIONS FOR LIVING THINKING IN THE TWENTY-FIRST CENTURY

Josie Alwyn celebrates the research journey underpinning Liz Attwell's pioneering work for education

[In which Josie and Liz explore: the formation of the etheric heart at adolescence and the quest for star knowledge; adolescence as a micro-reflection of the Fall; the possibility of a new clairvoyance and a new consciousness; an anthroposophical exploration of the a-ha moment; discovering the caduceus or staff of life; revivifying the senses and the world spiral; Steiner's exploration of the importance of the seventh seal as a pictorial representation of our path to fully realized humanity; the a-ha moment as overcoming duality and the subject/object divide to lead humanity back to unitary consciousness]

Editorial Preface

This chapter, which tracks the culminating years of Liz Attwell's educational research, from 2012 to 2019, has been brought together by Josie Alwyn from Liz's lecture notes, diary entries and from their many years of colleagueship and conversation. Liz herself guided this work until the very last days of her life.

During the years that Liz and I were a teaching team at Michael Hall Steiner School, as part of some memorably hilarious classroom drama activities with 15- and 16-year-old students, Liz thinly disguised us, the teachers, by renaming us, Messrs. Talwyn and Battwell. The composition of this chapter has been a wonderful opportunity for the team of Talwyn and Battwell to have one last innings and—unapologetically using the kind of pun that Liz enjoyed so much—for raising my glass to Battwell!

Chapter Introduction

At the end of her first two years of teaching A-level English Literature, Liz sat down in the summer holidays 2012 to write up her experience (described in Chapter Three) of her student group taking off and how building on the foundations they had established allowed their thinking to become brain-free in a consistent way that was breathtaking for all of them. 'We found ourselves looking at each other with (in Keats' words) "a wild surmise." Somehow, as a group: we were touching into the spirit.' This small act of self-reflection and review set in train the inner journey of her life.

She wrote:

> Everyone was free and not all of us were doing it all the time. However, collectively and over time, we were helping each other to develop our thinking. We were literally thinking 'outside the box' in ways that felt inspired. It felt as if we had created an etheric form, a sort of chalice, around the classroom table. There we experienced communion and community.
>
> Several students intimated that they sensed that what was happening was beyond the physical. To have drawn this awareness out would have been immoral in me as a teacher, though I was able to affirm what they expressed as direct perception.

Liz suggests, 'the concepts which lie behind this A-level Literature exam specification have been helpful in releasing an energy inherent in the study of literature as art. This is the dream of every teacher. I was experiencing it. In describing the "chalice" I was consciously referencing the College Imagination given to the teachers at the inauguration of the first Steiner school and spoken at Michael Hall before every College meeting:

> *We wish to form our thoughts in such a way that we may be conscious that:*
>
> *Behind each of us stands his Angel, gently laying his hands on the heads of each. This Angel gives you the strength which you need.*
>
> *Above your heads there sweep the circling Archangels. They carry from one to the other what each has to give the other. They unite your souls. Thereby you are given the courage of which you stand in need. (Out of this courage the Archangels form a chalice.)*
>
> *The light of wisdom is given to us by the exalted beings of the Archai, who are not limited to the circling movements, but who, coming forth from primal beginnings, manifest themselves and disappear into primal distances. They reveal themselves only in the form of a drop of light in this place. Into the chalice of courage there falls a drop of light, enlightening our times, bestowed by the ruling Spirit of our Age.*[1]

'This gives the dynamic of the three stages of consciousness that Steiner identifies in all his books as our way back to union with the spiritual world through Imagination, Inspiration and Intuition.'

When Liz writes, above, about the 'release of this energy inherent in the study of literature as art,' we note her description of the experience as one that is shared by everyone (teacher and students alike) when the conditions of a learning community are fulfilled in the classroom.

The experience is both individual and communal. The 17- and 18-year-old students express their experiences through their work; while Liz, their teacher, expresses her experience as a reflection of her work with the verse that Rudolf Steiner gave to the first College of Teachers—generally known as the *College Imagination*. As Liz writes, this reflection set in train the inner journey of her life. It also set in train a series of insights and revelations about the nature of teaching and learning processes that have profound implications for the realization of our humanity.

Liz's research journey has enabled her to penetrate the *College Imagination* in such a way that every educator, whatever their field, can follow and work out of Imagination, Inspiration and Intuition as a practical path of thinking, not only within oneself and for the education of children and young people *but also* for our collegial working together at educational development. In other words, Liz's path of thinking turns the *College Imagination* into something we can *do* for ourselves, for each other and for the world; and this is what we believe makes the conceptual journey of discovery that follows here a worthwhile reading experience.*

The Journey

That summer, 2012, Liz decided it was time to reconnect to the 'mothership' of the Anthroposophical Society. She had an extraordinary summer finding that 'other capacities are born' and she was trying to write down all her insights. Among them she 'realised the etheric heart' and, in the Michael Hall School summer inset day, described how 'thinking is taken down

---

* Knowledge of anthroposophical terms, such as can be found in Steiner's *The Education of the Child*, will help the reader follow this chapter.

The basic anthroposophical texts by Rudolf Steiner, *Occult Science* and *Knowledge of Higher Worlds* offer a recommended path of study: they are referred to, implicitly and explicitly, throughout the book.

The following collections of Rudolf Steiner's texts, edited with a specific focus on the path of Imagination, Inspiration and Intuition, are highly recommended as a resource for deepening understanding in this field and for further research:

1. *Heart Thinking: Inspired Knowledge* by Rudolf Steiner; selected and compiled by Martina Maria Sam; transl. Matthew Barton; Rudolf Steiner Press, 2017.

2. *Imagination: Enhancing the Powers of Thinking* by Rudolf Steiner; compiled and edited by Edward de Boer; transl. Matthew Barton; Rudolf Steiner Press, 2019.

3. *Intuition: The Focus of Thinking by Rudolf Steiner*; compiled and edited by Edward de Boer; transl. by J. Collis; Rudolf Steiner Press, 2019.

through the heart and inverts and comes back up, to inspired thought outside the head; how this lights up the constellations of stars which dimmed to make the etheric heart'[2]. She describes this in *Discovering the Etheric Heart*:

> Class 9 seems a time when students often 'come apart at the seams.' The perfect youths that the class teacher handed over disappear. In their place is loutish behaviour; the typical 'Kevin' character. Neuroscience tells us that brains are being rewired at this time. Students have little capacity for empathy; when shown pictures of faces showing emotion teenagers, at this point, are less able to correctly identify the emotion being conveyed than younger children. Everyone around them wonders what has gone wrong and whether it will come right.
>
> As a teacher of English, I always found this a challenging time. These teenagers seem to work against your best efforts, convinced that you are their worst enemy. Then, gradually, through Class 10 I would begin to see what I called 'the lights coming on.' Around the classroom I would see, one by one, an individuality looking back at me. Two eyes which belonged to someone who had begun to say to themselves: 'This is my life and I am responsible for it.' This was always a magical moment which signalled a change in our relationship from my being an authority to that of facilitator. Eventually, by the end of the year, most of the 'lights' would be on; if they weren't it often meant problems for that student in Class 11.

murn blue   ʔ///ʔ violet
//// orange ⊹⌐ yellow

Recently I have been trying to understand Steiner's description of the development of the etheric heart. Here are some thoughts stimulated by this concept.

Steiner describes the etheric heart as forming between the change of teeth and adolescence around the physical heart (a provisional etheric heart supplied by the forces 'inherent in the embryo'). The etheric body of the child at birth is 'a universe in the form of images', with in its circumference 'something like stars, and in its lower part something reveals itself which is more or less an image of the earth.' Steiner says that it also contains a 'sort of image of the sun and moon.' He describes how gradually these stars begin to ray inwards to form the new etheric heart. As they do they become pale, though still present.

////// yellow ///ɴ red
ɯ/ɯ blue ⌀ orange

Also culminating at puberty an astral structure forms around the etheric heart, within which is inscribed the actions of the individual. Steiner describes it thus: 'from puberty onwards the totality of man's actions pours, via the astral body, into the etheric heart.'

The 'I' slips into the lungs and from there, via the circulation, it enters the etheric/astral heart in such a way that 'the ideas on which we base our actions also become inscribed. In this way human karma unites with cosmic laws,' says Steiner.

Steiner continues; 'The real building up of karma only begins from the moment when the astral heart has fully penetrated the etheric heart, so that the two form a unity. One could say that this union constitutes, as it were, an organism for the forming of karma.' I experience this moment of 'the lights coming on' as being the moment that the individuality connects to this etheric/astral organ; it is rather like the clouds clearing away from the face of the sun. The main lessons in Class 10 feel designed to weave a cradle for the birth of this organ concentrating as they do on giving the individual foundations. Main lessons such as Myth into Literature and History of Art, for instance, are designed to answer the adolescent's question of 'what is the point?', not with a definitive answer, but with a sense for the long context within which this question has been asked over millennia.

Steiner strongly links this moment to the birth of a 'true power of judgement'; adding that 'not until then can the child begin to form real judgements of her/his own.'

Once this has happened, I experience a new possibility in the young person. Whatever content comes towards them they can take it in and down to the heart region where it can undergo a creative metamorphosis; turning inside out and upside down and then raying out from them back into the world. It seems to me that they begin to have the possibility to reconnect to the image of the cosmos in their etheric bodies, lighting up the images of the stars. In this raying I experience the young people as being able to connect with each other so that a touching in the spirit can come about, overcoming isolation; thus communion is achieved. When this happens tremendous learning and transformation take place.

Previously I had regarded teenagers as pre-ego and therefore less responsible for their actions. While I still think this is valid, I feel that the conception of the birth of a new organ at puberty which unites etheric, astral and ego makes the conscientious education of adolescents both more important and more exciting. How should we educate in the light of this knowledge?

As Steiner's verse says, given at Easter at the last education congress he attended in Stuttgart:

> Yielding to matter/ Is wasting of souls.
> Finding oneself in the spirit/ Is uniting of human beings.
> Beholding oneself in human beings/ Is building of worlds.

To accompany and participate in this transformation with young people is the enormous privilege of the Upper School teacher.'[3]

Liz further notes, 'in conversation with Josie Alwyn she pointed out that the hand movements that I was using to describe the whole process showed a turning at the bottom—and I realised that my hand gestures described a "response" from my students and not a "reaction." Which links to Steiner's diagram in Lecture 4 of *Life of the Human Soul and its Relation to World*

white ///// red

Evolution, where he says that thoughts are warmed by urges, desires, instincts, forces—this gives them a soul-colouring. Here Steiner describes that these impulses can be purified to achieve Imagination and Inspiration. Memories are the etheric stream *recalled up.* Inspirational thinking is the alchemy of the soul. Cold thought passed through the heart into the cauldron of the desires and instincts, connecting with purified warmth, rises up to light up the stars of the cosmic etheric body to create a "firmament fretted with golden fire" [*Hamlet*].'[4]

Here, then, we have a dynamic picture of the journey of the human soul towards star knowledge.

The Star Knowledge

Someone who worked with literature and the levels of Imagination, Inspiration and Intuition[*] in teaching was W.J. Stein. In his Preface to *The Ninth Century and the Holy Grail,* Stein writes:

> The adolescent youth, at the age of 15 or 16, needs the firm sense of the earth. Between 16 and 17 however, he must reconquer the worlds of the stars, but now as one who stands established upon the earth. If this possibility is taken away from him, he is delivered over to all the suffering that comes from the forces of an ungoverned physical nature. Those alone fall a prey to greed or passion who cannot in innocent purity rise above the bodily nature to the world of the stars. The subject-matter of the eleventh class provides for this need... The pupil realises that sympathy must be found again through knowledge; that love and pity must be felt for everything in the whole world. In this way the growing youth becomes free from his body. We have a citizen of the wide universe, so that he may learn—as Herder says—to feel the earth as a 'star amongst stars.'[5]

This is echoed in the inherent journey of Rudolf Steiner's well-known verse:

The Stars spake once to Man
It is World-destiny

---

* Helpful explanations of the use of capital letters for Imagination, Inspiration and Intuition can be found in Steiner's *Occult Science,* and among other places, in the Introduction to *Imagination, Enhancing Powers of Thinking,* Rudolf Steiner Press, 2019 [translator's note, p.1].

Also see, for example, *ch. 4 Understanding Imagination Through Inspiration and Intuition, ibid, p. 84*

That they are silent now.
To be aware of this silence
Can become pain for earthly Man.

But in the deepening silence
There grows and ripens
What Man speaks to the stars.
To be aware of this speaking
Can become strength for Spirit-Man.

Liz writes, 'later in the book Stein makes this more explicit and links it to the young Parzival in Wolfram von Eschenbach's c.1201 epic of that name—where Wolfram's ultimate source is the star writing:

> It is just this that is lacking in Parzival—he cannot read star-writing, he does not find the words that are inscribed on the Grail sword, he only looks at what is revealed to him in Imagination, he does not rise to the reading of this picture-writing, to *Inspiration*. What the human being sees when he enters the Grail Castle is himself. It is precisely this knowledge that the Grail seeker must acquire, that no one else can answer the question for him when his own being confronts him and asks, 'Brother, what is wrong with thee?' No one else can answer this question—only he himself can do it. For the answer to this Parzival-question is, 'I myself have caused all this suffering that I see here."[6]

Liz concludes, 'What Wolfram describes is a central moment in any human being's life and can be linked to the successful birth of the etheric heart in adolescence.'

The ancient wisdom of this archetypal journey of the human life is inherent to Wolfram's entire narrative of Parzival's life journey: it is only after years of quest and bitter experience, following his first abject failure at the castle of the Grail, that Parzival will find he has made up for what he then lacked. This is not so much self-discovery as a moment of epiphany brought to him by others' reading the star writing on the Grail itself. In Wolfram's story, it is Cundrie, the messenger of the Grail at Mon Salvasche, who finds and publicly delivers to Parzival the news of his recognition, in the following words:

> The Inscription has been read: you are to be Lord of the Grail! ... your truthful lips are now to address noble, gentle King Anfortas and with their Question banish his agony and heal him, who could equal you in bliss?
> Seven stars [Cundrie] named in Arabic. They were known to the noble potentate Feirefiz who sat before her... 'Now take note, Parzival,' she said.[7] 'I do not pronounce it in a dream: these planets are the bridle of the firmament, checking its onrush; their contrariness ever ran counter to its momentum. You have now abandoned care. All that the planets embrace within their orbits,

whatever they shed light on, marks the scope of what it is for you to attain and achieve. Your sorrow is doomed to pass away—greed alone can deny you your portion. The Grail and its power forbid false companionship. You raised a brood of cares in tender years: but the happiness which is on its way to you has dashed their expectations. You have won through to peace of soul and outlived cares to have joy of your body.[8]

We note the precision of the wording here: in front of all King Arthur's court Cundrie assures Parzival that the Inscription on the Grail has been read and that it reads true: that what she says is not to be taken just as in some dream but is objective truth. Indeed, the planets are already known to Parzival's older brother from the East, noble Feirefiz. These planets are the 'bridle of the firmament'; and now 'all that the planets embrace within their orbits, whatever they shed light on, marks the scope of what it is for [Parzival] to attain and achieve.'

The imagery of chivalry and horsemanship—of the uses of bridles and reins and the relationship with one's horse—has been a potent metaphor for the individual's changing relationship to the world, throughout Wolfram's story. It has been leading us from Parzival's most ignorant and ignoble acquisition of the Red Knight's horse in early adolescence [Book 3] to this most noble recognition of Parzival's mature achievement of true inner sovereignty in the epic's penultimate chapter [Book 15].

Through the star writing that has appeared on the Grail and the picture that Cundrie's reading of it paints, the implication is clear: Parzival is now invited to take what he has learned of earthly chivalric skills into the starry cosmos; to take up the reins in a realm whose scope is marked by 'all that the planets embrace within their orbits, whatever they shed light on,' that is, to experience the joy of consciously understanding and working as co-creator in dynamic harmony with the planets, 'the bridle of the firmament, checking its onrush.' Thus, in c.1201, Wolfram describes the pathway through Imagination to Inspiration and rising 'to the reading of this picture-writing,' to Intuition. Wolfram's imagery is unique but its dynamic is the same as the *College Imagination* given centuries later by Rudolf Steiner to help teachers work together in the education of children and young people.

The Fall

The narratives of this archetypal human journey towards star knowledge begin with a Fall. In Genesis, the fall from innocence happens when Adam and Eve eat the apple from the Tree of Knowledge and become self-conscious. Established interpretations of this narrative are quite fixed, but there are alternatives to be found; as, for example, this well-known Medieval English lyric:

> *Adam lay bounden,*
> *Bounden in a bond:*
> *Four thousand winter*
> *Thought he not too long.*
> *And all was for an apple,*
> *And apple that he tok,*
> *As clerkes finden*
> *Written in here book.*
>
> *Ne hadde the apple take ben*
> *The apple taken ben,*
> *Ne hadde never our Lady*
> *A ben Hevene Quen.*
> *Blissed be the time*
> *That apple take was!*
> *Therefore we mourn singer,*
> *'Deo gracias!'*[9]

The dynamic here is the necessity of 'falling' in order to rise: just as the fledgling bird must take courage and fall from the nest in order to find its wings and fly. Therefore, says the lyric, 'Thank God, for the Fall!'

This fall from innocence can be associated, in individual development, with the onset of puberty. In 1928, Erich Gabert, a primary school teacher who had worked with Steiner, wrote about puberty initiating the transformative process of adolescence as a microcosmic reflection of the Fall:

> The young teenager 'cannot bear that others probe his feelings, even though in younger years it never mattered. Now he knows that he would hate to show his feelings and desires to any other person, even though he often feels driven to reveal them. Nevertheless, he will always hold back what is pre-eminently his inmost core; those feelings he must hide from everyone. And so, what was earlier all openness is now a completely closed-in entity. This inner, sensitive presence is what we call 'soul'; it has slowly taken on a separate existence and become an interior world, in which the personality can live when it is not connected with outside things. Here, one's most inward perceptions can be cherished as well as one's secret awareness of evil and—perhaps even more—of good.
>
> A particular element of this inner life is the feeling that it is closed away in itself, so that anyone who tries to peer in must be repulsed. This produces the very delicate, subtle feeling of shame that is characteristic of this age.

Something like a protective shell holds and conceals what is beginning to grow within like a tender plant. This is the process that Rudolf Steiner calls the 'birth of the astral soul-nature of the human being'; it is the process of becoming an independent personality. It means the severing of the bonds that held the younger child in an unconscious relationship with his environment and with the people around him.

The pain of the young person is caused by his feelings of antipathy and the breaking away from the earlier attachment to his own small world. Actually, it is this that makes it possible for him to apprehend himself as a separate person, a 'self.' Not that a younger child, too, cannot feel himself as a separate self, but in adolescence the development takes on such a suddenly new and different character that one is able to recognize the quality of a primary step in the pre-teen.

The forces of antipathy in adolescence, besides isolating his inner life in a kind of shell, have another highly significant effect on the young person. When he looks out over the newly built wall around his dwelling-place—his 'self'—he sees the outside world in an entirely new light. Not only has he stepped back from the objects and persons outside, but he also finds that in doing this he can see much more clearly than before. His earlier attachments and feelings of oneness had allowed only an unconscious, undifferentiated knowledge; now there occurs a gradual awakening. He can, by detaching himself from the world around him, perceive it; before, when he was within that world, he could only feel it. This is the process that brings understanding to birth. Just as the judge in court can only decide a case when he is not involved on either side but sits above and over the proceedings, the teenager, having drawn away from his former world, is now able to acquire the capacity of judgement. A future creative thinking is in preparation. This is its foundation.[10]

If we set Gabert's description of the process that brings understanding to birth, alongside Steiner's description of the heart's transformation in adolescence, we have before us a multi-layered picture of this phase of the human soul's journey: its fall into self-consciousness alongside its potential to rise again on individually-fashioned wings of self-knowledge and empathic imagination. It is a poignantly conflicted yearning, both for the lost paradisal home and for individual freedom from it, that characterizes this phase of human development. The last words of Milton's *Paradise Lost*, seem to find their reflection in every reader's heart: when Adam and Eve, first exiled from Paradise leave it behind them:

> *Some natural tears they dropped, but wiped them soon:*
> *The world was all before them, where to choose*
> *Their place of rest, and providence their guide:*
> *They hand in hand with wandering steps and slow,*
> *Through Eden took their solitary way.'*[11]

Finding the Way

In the context of the Fall and the freedom it opens up for each individual to develop their own inner potential, Jeremy Naydler has written of the 'challenge of addressing the hunger that humanity feels so strongly for greater connection with the realm of the Spirit, and which many mistakenly seek to satisfy through greater connection to technology.'[12] Individual freedom of choice in such a powerfully seductive world as ours contains many, often invisible, pitfalls. Liz, however, turns the challenge another way, perceiving the technological creations of our Fallen world as pictures of spiritual possibility if we can find the way to see it:

> In Genesis, the Garden of Paradise has the Tree of Life and the Tree of Knowledge of Good and Evil. Lucifer tempts Eve and when Adam eats the apple he feels naked—self-conscious. This is the astral body entering too early. So, as self-consciousness is the effect of the Fall, the sickness from which we suffer now is the result of self-consciousness. What we've done in a Fallen way is usually offering a picture of spiritual possibility. For example, the Internet can be seen as a Fallen Akashic Record. The spiritual comes first and then is grabbed by the lower beings: the dragon of Revelation tries to take away the baby from the woman who is birthing it:—us![13]

In other words, as a result of 'the astral body entering too early', the human being is continually in danger of drowning in this dream-like astral realm of swirling desires, illusions and delusions; where humans are subject to all the extreme weathers of emotion striving to drag them down into the lowest depths. At the beginning of Shakespeare's *Twelfth Night*, the lovesick Duke Orsino addresses this overwhelming experience:

> *O spirit of love, how quick and fresh art thou,*
> *That notwithstanding thy capacity*
> *Receiveth as the sea, naught enters there,*
> *Of what validity and pitch so e'er,*
> *But falls into abatement and low price*
> *Even in a minute! So full of shapes is fancy*
> *That it alone is high fantastical.*[14]

Orsino does learn to steer the stormy seas of the astral realm and to penetrate the delusions of surface appearances recognizing, in his very last words of the play, that Viola is his true love and his 'Fancy's Queen'.[15] She is the sovereign being through whose recognition troubled waters are calmed and tuned to a living harmony. His belated recognition of Viola not only inaugurates a 'golden time' in Orsino's world, but also provides wonderful moments of epiphany for playgoers. Until, that is, Feste ends

Twelfth Night in the rain; which seems here to represent the dismal post-celebration realities of mundane life. Is Shakespeare suggesting that our experience of Twelfth Night (the play and the festival of Epiphany) depends, as it does for his characters, upon our way of seeing the world? Can we ever reach our own calm shore and inaugurate a golden time unless, as Orsino does so memorably, we learn how to see through the surface appearance of daily life and recognize the truth that lies hidden within?

This theme of seeing differently, of paying attention to 'the opening of the inner eye', is not a new learning path though, from many points of view, 'now seems like a good time' to attend to it.[16] In a diary entry near the end of 2012, Liz captures in one intuitive nutshell the insights that unfold over the following years in her work and in this essay:

> To return we must perceive below the surface of things—to penetrate to an awareness of the etheric in the moment. This is a pillar—within us—poured into the physical body all the time. We perceive the material world but we begin to have direct percepts from the spiritual world—this is where Intuition always comes from; and is also percept-forming whole.[17] This is the Tree of Life.'[18]
>
> She goes on to cite Steiner, in 1907, describing how the training that can transform the Tree of Knowledge in us into the flourishing Tree of Life takes place in the etheric body[19]. It is Goethe's 'scientific approach that offers the basic building block of such genuine, experience-based enquiry'.[20]:
>
> If he had written a book Goethe would give us an archetypal model of how to find the laws of objective contemplation of the world'.[21]

Goethe's phenomenological approach, as elucidated in earlier chapters of this book, is a training in the art of thinking and imagination; which allows us to retune our human sensitivities and capabilities in the service of nature and truth. His method, widely practiced in fields of Steiner Waldorf education, relies on building up objective observation of phenomena in stages.

The first stage is observing what is objectively, materially there before us in space. The second stage moves to observation in time: requiring us to perceive below the material surface of things, through a disciplined use of imagination to 'see' the phenomenon as part of a living process in a context, taking part of its form from its environment. Practising this second stage develops an objective awareness of the etheric world, the realm of flowing life forces that have formative power through time: biological cycles of life, the tides of the sea, the habits and rhythms humans live by, our powers of memory and imagination all have to do with the etheric realm. This disciplining of imagination strengthens our individual faculties of inspiration and intuition and enables the development of Imagination, Inspiration and Intuition.

Liz explains that:

> when you've been looking at the phenomena for a long time, concentrating on the phenomena without judgement, then, suddenly, there is Imagination. Steiner says the old clairvoyance was given to us by the Spirits of Form who presented us with tableaux, visions and dream visions. But this is the new clairvoyance that you have to work for: you work at concentrating on the phenomenon without judgement, to make yourself a channel just for the phenomenon—you don't engage speculative thinking. It's Keats' 'negative capability' (no 'irritable reaching after fact and reason'—no cause and effect thinking). Then you suddenly begin to see the answers arriving from behind you, from the 'back space" and you're 'reading' them. This is Inspiration and it is given to you by a different set of beings. Steiner talks about the new clairvoyance coming from Spirits of Personality with whom one has to actively engage, through concentrated objective observation of the phenomenon already described, to receive inspiration. If we work hard at observing outer phenomena, then the answer comes to us from behind. One can experience inspiration coalescing in our back space and, with practice, recognise it as a kind of 'mandala', which forms up like a kaleidoscope in our back space, and that one can 'read' in the same way that one reads a feeling—'reading the hidden script' is like reading feeling. So, you can see the phenomena rising up, as it were, in front of you while, from behind, you can 'see' the concepts coming towards you from the back space'.

---

* As Liz died without completing her work, there have been some points where we have not been able to ask her for a definition of the concepts she was working with. Lesley Forward, a Eurythmist, gave a fuller picture of the back space:

> Imagine a human being standing up straight; in front of them is what can be perceived, the visible, material world. They are looking forwards, into the future. Behind them, in the back space, is invisible; it cannot be perceived with the eye, it is the spiritual dimension. It is the past. If we say that someone is an upright person, we are already pointing to both the inner and outer dimensions: firstly, their physical posture and also their moral quality.
>
> In ancient Greece, the Herma were standing stones with carved heads (often of the Greek god, Hermes) which were used to mark boundaries. Likewise, each human being is a boundary marker; between the past and the future, the invisible and the visible. They are the boundary between the material and spiritual worlds. Hermes too is a conduit between worlds between the conscious and unconscious and is inextricably linked with Hermes Trismegestus.
>
> Eurythmy continually weaves on this boundary between two worlds, in that it makes visible through gesture invisible spiritual forces. When Liz spoke about the back space, she was referring to the spiritual dimension.

Liz has observed the experience of revelation in students as sometimes being so powerful that 'the eyes bulge, because Inspiration is just coming through them; flowing through them from behind. And that is why,' she concludes, 'students can start waving their arms about in the classroom, because a lot of excitement and energy is being generated. The brain lights up before the students actually see the answers; and then it comes through and they blurt it out, usually all at once.'[22] She writes in her diary, 'Is a new capacity being born? Shown outwardly by the development of internet information overlaying our perceptions of the world?—a Fallen reflection of a new ability to tune into the inner etheric activity of the soul?'[23]

Practising Goethe's phenomenological approach 'builds up observation and facts until you can move through the frozen moments in time, backwards and forwards, to experience a whole phenomenon—a whole plant or a whole Shakespeare play— in movement.'[24] 'As we consider a text' writes Steiner, 'pictures and ideas take shape in our spirit, that seem to be called forth, to be created by the text.'[25] So, Liz notes, 'The structure of texts can be read just like bones, to find spiritual realities within.'[26]

An example of this archetypal human thinking process is taken from the twentieth/twenty-first century global bestseller, *His Dark Materials* by Philip Pullman, who is described as one of those writers who emerge once in a lifetime, and 'is so extraordinary that the imagination of generations is altered'.[27] This hugely popular, acclaimed and still unfolding epic tale[28] also revolves around questions of human consciousness, freedom of thought and expression and of how to 'read' the truth beyond the surface of things—almost as if it is meeting and responding to a need of our times.

One ingenious creation of Pullman's imagination is the 'alethiometer': a rare, beautiful and intricate device of Lyra's world which works mysteriously as a compass in the realm of truth. Lyra, the main character, has an exceptional and natural gift for reading the alethiometer's pictorial language; and while she is a child she can read the truth it tells with ease and grace. In some episodes we can gently unpick the closely woven narrative and come quite close to reading the writer's underlying intentions. There is a relevant example in *The Subtle Knife*[29], where Pullman juxtaposes three different kinds of devices created for discovering truths below the surface: the I Ching, the digital computer and the alethiometer:

Lyra, guided by the alethiometer, is exploring, for the first time, a parallel Oxford-world to her own and arrives, unannounced, at the science laboratory of Dr Mary Malone: a physicist who is using computer technology to research the 'dark matter' of the universe—not the visible stars and planets, but the invisible 'stuff' that makes 'it all to hang together'[30]. She has found that, by developing the poet Keats' 'negative capability' in herself she has not only discovered a way to see these invisible 'Shadow particles', but also found that they are conscious; that 'they answer back'—but, and this is the part that is unbelievable for her, only if 'you know that they are there.' All of Dr Malone's training in material science is challenged by this discovery and will not allow her to recognize the truth of her own observations and experience.

Lyra, however, immediately recognizes both the process by which Dr Malone has made her discovery and the truth of it. By using her own 'negative capability' to demonstrate how the pictorial language of the alethiometer works—showing her the true answers provided through her 'conversation' with these 'particles of Dark Matter'—Lyra persuades Dr Malone to let her try it out on the computer. Digital technology is new to Lyra although, as Dr Malone sets up the wiring and the computer with all its electronic humming and lights and switches, Lyra is reminded of the cruelly evil use of such technologies in her world, to cut children from their daemons, with the justification that it is for their own good. Nevertheless, she bravely confronts the computer's blank screen and, as a creative experiment to see if it will work, simply imagines she is following the same thinking process by which she reads her alethiometer. It works and the success of her computer demonstration astonishes Dr Malone, enabling Lyra to suggest to her the huge potential for developing the research with computer technology using this power of creative imagination in human consciousness[31]. Lyra also learns, by successfully transferring her alethiometer 'reading' skills to the computer, that there must be 'lots of ways' of truth-reading, when previously she had thought there was only the alethiometer. The I Ching is another way; a way which Dr Malone later goes on to develop when she finds herself in a world without computer technology.

Lyra can't understand why people in her world hate these invisible 'particles' of Dark Matter: 'They want to destroy it. They think it's evil. But I think what *they* do is evil. I seen them do it.'[32] Dr Malone, who had previously lived as a nun and had chosen to leave behind those 'superstitious beliefs' to practice science, is seriously 'embarrassed' by Lyra's reference to ideas of good and evil in the context of a scientific research laboratory and refuses to think about it. But 'You got to think about it,' said Lyra severely. 'You can't investigate Shadows, Dust, whatever it is, without thinking about that kind of thing, good and evil and such. [..] You can't refuse.'[33] Perhaps it is Lyra's proven moral integrity that adds such authoritative weight to her insistence that Dr Malone must include thinking about good and evil in her scientific method. This, her first, meeting with Lyra changes the whole direction of Dr Malone's life and work; ultimately enabling her to use the full range of her human potential to change, not only her world, but all worlds, on a macrocosmic scale—she is portrayed achieving the greatest good for the cosmos through her role in the healing of human consciousness.[34] In our present episode, through the meeting of different ways of thinking represented by Lyra Silvertongue and Mary Malone, I think Pullman is demonstrating, not only the vastly superior power of human imagination over digital technology, but also suggesting the beneficial potential of digital technology if it is guided by *all* the powers of human consciousness; perhaps above all, by the power of moral imagination. This episode of *The Subtle Knife* above echoes William Blake's idea that 'Everything possible to be believ'd is an image of truth' and, thus, sets us off on a journey of imaginative thinking that will marvellously unfold through all the succeeding volumes of Philip Pullman's great epic of human consciousness[35].

For Pullman, 'stories are the most important thing in the world. Without stories, we wouldn't be human beings at all.'[36] In his championing freedom of thinking and expression, he not only makes Lyra a natural storyteller, but also creates his whole universe out of literary 'energy': the term 'His Dark Materials' is, of course, from Milton's *Paradise Lost*. He calls the computer the Cave[37], explicitly referring to Plato's cave, where human beings who try to read the meaning of shadows that are reflected by the fire's light on the cave walls mistake them for revelations of sunlit truth, that can only be discovered by leaving the cave for the world outside. Plato begs the question, why do some human beings prefer to stay with shadows of the truth in the darkness of the cave, imprisoned by their own deluded thinking, when they could simply turn around and walk out into the beautiful sunlit world of true freedom outside? It is a significant question for our time and is raised to powerful effect through the medium of story—the popularity of Pullman's writing is enabling it to reach hearts and minds across the world. I think Pullman could hardly be suggesting more clearly that the path to the kind of truth that can set human beings free for action, is through imaginative, inspired, creative thinking that consciously includes understanding good and evil.

The extended commentary, above, on works of literature ranging from the twelfth to the twenty-first centuries, is to demonstrate that 'the energy inherent in the study of literature as an art' is in the act of writing as much as in the study of it. It is an energy inherent in all creative engagement with literary art. Through their depth of engagement readers and writers are enabled to strike through the surface of consciousness and discover latent powers within, which brought to expression can serve our most fundamental human needs.

In the context of young people's education in the twenty-first century and of Liz's experience of the new capacities being born in them, it is notable that her students' way of learning using Goethe's approach and Lyra's way of reading the alethiometer are so strikingly similar. Both writers use precisely the same words of Keats to describe the 'negative capability' necessary for seeing below the surface of things; and, among many other examples, in his most recent *Book of Dust* trilogy, Pullman has the 11-year-old Malcolm Polstead in a significant kind of Socratic dialogue with the scholar, Dr Hannah Relf, about the different ways of thinking involved in the language of symbolic pictures and that of Pythagoras' theorem[38]; suggesting a similarity of approach to the education of young people for which Liz Attwell and her research are celebrated here. Liz's deep engagement with the work of Rudolf Steiner in this field has the potential for enabling a great renewal in the art of education, through rediscovering the vital role of teaching and learning processes for the healing of our humanity. Her perception of the new capacities developing in young people, to tune into the inner etheric activity of the soul, and her pioneering work to support them, led her to a reading of what underpins her students' revelatory learning experiences.

An Anthroposophical Reading of the A-ha Moment

'So,' said Liz, 'what lies behind the experience of the a-ha moment?

'In describing normal consciousness, one picture I have come to, along with others, is a circle that describes the periphery of a certain field of experience: the boundary between the outer and inner self [see next page]. Florian Osswald[39] used this drawing to suggest going out to the boundaries to find the phenomenon, really attending deeply to the pure phenomenon.

He then added a lemniscate and the terms "percept" and "concept"[40]. The idea being, he explained, that you need to go out to the very edge of the field to really experience the pure phenomenon and you also need the opportunity to return inwardly if you are to get a sense of the concept. He sees it as two wings. You must have a balance: if one of these wings is not in balance with the other there is a laming, or one-sidedness, going on [see second image, over].

'Another speaker, Michael Brinch[41], added to this picture: "It is the baby", he said, "who goes out to the pure percept and is looking to build his or her concepts up. This rhythm between the experience of the percept and the concept is how we learn". I call it the Lemniscate of Learning. Michael Brinch shows that as we develop and have learnt some concepts, we don't always go right out to the "percept" edge. We make assumptions. We have to do that because we can't always be like babies experiencing astonishing

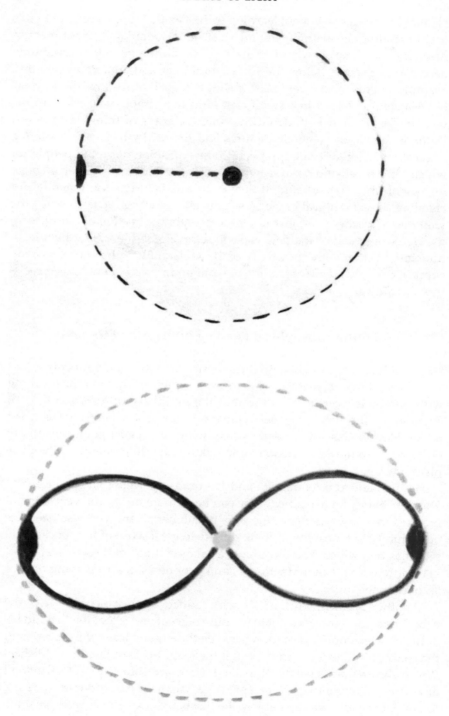

phenomena. We haven't got the energy. So, in a certain sense, having learnt to know that a "table" is just a "table"; we don't have to have a new experience of that phenomenon each time. We don't have to go back to the original concept all the time—Michael Brinch explains that we often have a sort of secondhand concept:

'You can see the negative potential of this inner lemniscate, which can be called the lemniscate of fundamentalism. Michael Brinch describes how these people, who think in fundamentalist ways, don't go back to perceive the phenomenon anew. A healthy person will go back sometimes to the edge of the field, to the original pure phenomenon-to the edge of one's boundaries as it were—in order to have a chance to have new concepts, new ideas and ways of thinking. If you reduce the lemniscate you make generalized assumptions—obviously, for example, in religious or racial prejudice. You can end up with a very small lemniscate [see over], where you're not going to get back to the edge of the field at all.

'Now I want to turn to the experiences I'd been having doing A-level English literature with my students; where they were having immense events that they themselves called a-ha moments. The name actually came from the students at the end-of-year review. They said, "We had so many a-ha moments" and I wondered, "What's an a-ha moment?" It

is certainly characterized by having attended to phenomena intensely, having worked at something for a long time, a text for example, and perhaps having slept on it. Then, just before the a-ha moment, when the idea actually arrives, one can observe in oneself that breathing becomes more rapid and the heart rate increases. Once I started recognizing the symptoms in my students I began to see them more and more. I would urge everyone to look out for the symptoms in others and in themselves; to check out how it feels and pay attention because these phenomena are very significant: the life processes are enlivened through the activity and through the senses. Tremendous[42] energy is being released. The students would blurt out what they'd "seen" and then everyone else in the room would become very energized by what was being said—the conversation would spiral upwards and tremendous learning was going on. I had very little to do with it, I was just observing what was going on. It was the students who saw what they were talking about and took it up for themselves. Subsequently they'd drum their feet on the floor and we'd get complaints from the teachers next door about the noise we were making! People would start shouting, making ringing noises, all sorts of strange things.

'My next thought was, how does this relate to what I call the Lemniscate of Learning described above? For William Wordsworth, the

phenomena of "Daffodils" can "flash up on the inward eye" when rec-
ollected in tranquility and we can develop our concept. But I was feeling something different and I tried to draw it. The first thing I drew in
my diary was me standing:

'And when I have an a-ha moment I feel transfixed between the percept
arising in front of me and the concept, which I experience, from behind
coming towards me. They meet in me: I become the portal between these
two ways.

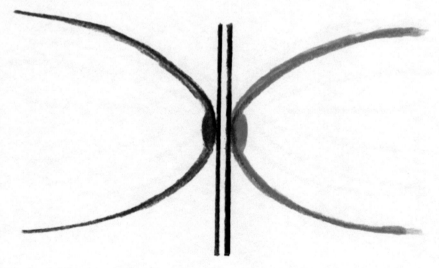

'In my picture, there's the percept and the concept and me in the middle, which I drew with a wiggly line because of the experience of energy that's released.

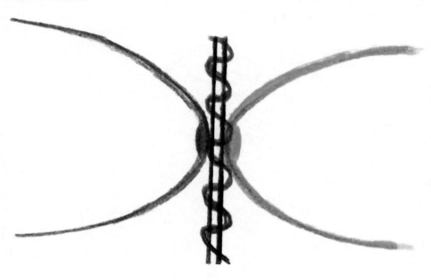

'In my next attempt at drawing my experience, I drew a dynamic "streaming out" from either side of the percept and the concept, which are fused in the middle. This represents my sense of streaming out to experience wide expanses of Space and Time in the a-ha moment.

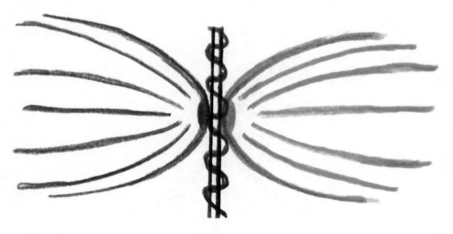

'The percept exists in Space. The concept, in some unfathomable way, comes from the primal beginnings of Time. So, in this moment I seemed to be able to see further. This was also happening to my students: they could see further than they had seen before, not infinite yet, but it was the beginnings of something significant about "seeing" that they were experiencing. And then I found lectures where Steiner talks about how, in these moments of Intuition, on the Space side there is a "coming in" of Imagination, moral imagination (the percept side)—from the higher self, that is normally only experienced after death. And on the Time side (the concept side) there is a "coming in" of Inspirations—and these come from before we were born.

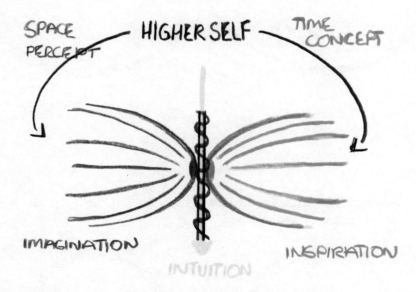

'When I listened to my students' certainty in those moments, I thought, "How do they know this is true? How do they know what they are seeing is true?" And the only way I could figure it out came to me: "It's because they knew it before they were born." They knew these things and they forgot them. And now they've rediscovered them. In one of three lectures on *Supersensible Man: Free Will and the Immortality of the Soul*, Steiner talks about the way the higher self, that normally lives outside of us, in these moments can enter and manifest in the world through pushing forward towards the gate of death; it's driving you onward to discover things. And in this a-ha moment, when everything inverts and turns inside out, it lifts up to moral imagination—this moral imagination that comes from what you would only meet after death. At the same time, it can be met by the Inspiration that is coming from what you knew before you were born. In between a drop of light comes down which is Intuition. Steiner says that Intuition is the kind of cognition that is of the utmost light-filled clarity—a cognition that carries with it absolute assurance of its validity. And that is what characterizes an a-ha moment: the knowledge that the new understanding has validity.

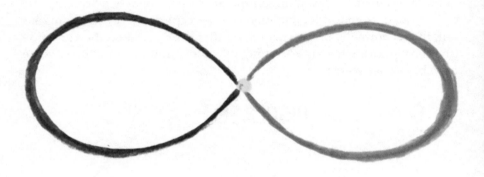

'Looking at this drawing, I could see that the two "ends" of the lemniscate-wings have lifted up.

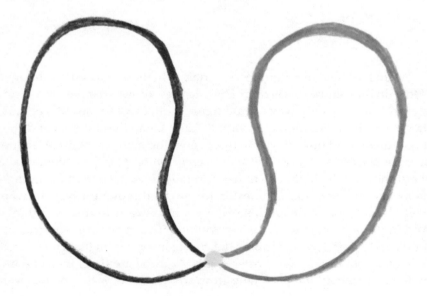

'They have lifted up into an "harmonious 8" form: a form given to Eurythmists, apparently related to the heart.* [43] And then Intuition, as a drop of light, comes down through the middle.

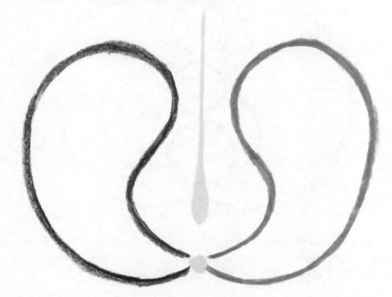

'In summary, we see the two wings of the percept and the concept. Then, suddenly, the whole thing comes up like a chalice and inverts; and they meet in you. So it's like standing in the middle. The physical phenomena come up "in front" of you, the concepts come up from behind; and you become the meeting place between the subject and the object—and that's the mystical moment of the unity; of the overcoming of the subject-object divide. And there is a release of energy, of joy from the heart, there's an immense amount of cerebral activity and your will engages.

---

* As explained by Lesley Forward; in Eurythmy, the horizontal figure 8 is a form initially polarized with two separate centres. As it seeks to become a whole, a complete unity, the crossover point drops down and the two sides or 'wings' of the form lift up and curve themselves around to fit inside a circle; thus forming a harmonious 8, a chalice. The harmonious 8 is hollow. It has an outside and an inside, like an organ. It can be seen as an image of the heart and circulatory system in which the blood rhythmically streams out through the body and back into the centre. The gesture of the harmonious 8 is of love that streams out into the world and dives back in to the centre to renew itself, like the pulse.

'Then I read further, about the life forces that spiral upwards:

'The life forces that start at the base of the spine and which, through your inner activity re-enliven you in the twelve senses. I realised I was looking at the Caduceus:*

'Thus, through the process of observing a-ha moments in my students and attempting to draw what I observed and was experiencing myself, I had ultimately arrived at the Caduceus, which is known as the Staff of Life and also the Tree of Life. The Caduceus is the sign of Hermes Trismegistus: the thrice majestic being of hermetic knowledge who can lead us into the spiritual world.'

---

*   In conversation with Catherine Fenton, Liz had described noting 'in my Diary January 2016: the double Helix as a pictorial microcosm of the Tree of Life, so I start finding that sort of thing out—including the Apprentice Pillar in the Roslyn Chapel which is said to contain the Holy Grail, is carved as a double helix in the form of the Tree of Life—and then, on 20 August 2016: I come to the Rod of Hermes: the wings denoting the higher self, there is the turning inside out; there is the fusing of subject and object and becoming co-creators with God. And there is the energy that's spiralling upwards. There are the two bits: the lemniscate coming up to make that energy, then this Kundalini energy that's coming up from the spine.'

Revivifying the Senses: the World Spiral

All of Liz's thoughts above, that now 'lead us into the spiritual world', are backed up in two major lecture series by Steiner—*The Life of the Human Soul* and *The Riddle of Humanity*—in which our microcosmic human activity is set on a macrocosmic stage of starry proportions.[44] To read them is to reorient ourselves amidst the completely other perspectives of the heavenly worlds; and to learn, like Parzival, how 'the planets are the bridle of the firmament'.

Coenraad van Houten based his work on learning processes on these lectures by Steiner; an extract from which is included below to help ground the reader amidst the vast pictures to follow:

The Seven Life Processes

A detailed description of the life processes may be found in Rudolf Steiner's lectures on *The Riddle of Humanity*. The following is a quotation from the lecture of 12 August 1916. We are starting from the assumption that all learning is first taken in through the senses:

> The situation of these powers of perception is different from the situation of forces that could be said to reside more deeply embedded within us. Seeing is bound up with the eyes and these constitute a particular region of a human being. Hearing is bound up with the organs of hearing, at least principally so, but it needs more besides—hearing involves much more of the organism than just the ear, which is what is normally thought of as the region of hearing. And life flows equally through each of these regions of the senses. The eye is alive, the ear is alive, that which is the foundation of all the senses is alive; the basis of touch is alive—all of it is alive. Life resides in all the senses; it flows through all the regions of the senses.
>
> If we look more closely at this life, it also proves to be differentiated. There is not just one life process. And you must also distinguish what we have been calling the sense of life, through which we perceive our own vital state, from the subject of our present discussion. What I am talking about now is the very life that flows through us. That life also differentiates itself within us. It does so in the following manner. The twelve regions of the twelve senses are to be pictured as being static, at rest within the organism. But life pulsates through the whole organism, and this life is manifested in various ways. First of all there is breathing, a manifestation of life necessary to all living things. Every living organism must enter into a breathing relationship with the external world. Today I cannot go into the details of how this differs for animals, plants and human beings, but will only point out that every living thing must have its breathing. The breathing of human beings is perpetually being

renewed by what they take in from the outer world, and this benefits all the regions associated with the senses. The sense of smell could not manifest itself—neither sight, nor the sense of tone—if the benefits of breathing did not enliven it. Thus, I must assign 'breathing' to every sense. We breathe—that is one process—but the benefits of that process of breathing flow to all the senses.

The second process we can distinguish is warming. This occurs along with breathing but is a separate process. Warming, the inner process of warming something through, is the second of the life-sustaining processes. The third process that sustains life is nourishment. So here we have three ways in which life comes to us from without: breathing, warming, nourishing. The outer world is part of each of these. Something must be there to be breathed—in the case of humans, and also animals, that substance is air. Warming requires a certain amount of warmth in the surroundings; we interact with it. Just think how impossible it would be for you to maintain proper inner warmth if the temperature of your surroundings were much hotter or much colder. If it were one hundred degrees lower your warmth processes would cease, they would not be possible; at one hundred degrees hotter you would do more than just sweat! Similarly, we need food to nourish us as long as we are considering the life processes in their earthly aspects.

At this stage, the life processes take us deeper into the internal world. We now find processes that re-form what has been taken in from outside—processes that transform and internalise it. To characterize this re-forming, I would like to use the same expressions that we have used on previous occasions. Our scientists are not yet aware of these things and therefore have no names for them, so we must formulate our own. The purely inner process that is the basis of the re-forming of what we take in from outside us can be seen to be fourfold.

Following the process of nourishing, the first internal process is the process of secretion, of elimination. When the nourishment we have taken in is distributed to our body, this is already the process of secretion; through the process of secretion it becomes part of our organism. The process of elimination does not just work outwards, it also separates out that part of our nourishment that is to be absorbed into us. Excretion and absorption are two sides of the processes by which organs of secretion deal with our nourishment. One part of the secretion performed by organs of digestion separates out nutriments by sending them into the organism. Whatever is thus secreted into the organism must remain connected with the life processes, and this involves a further process which we will call maintaining. But for there to be life, it is not enough for what is taken in to be maintained, there also must be growth. Every living thing depends on a process of inner growth: a process of growth, taken in the widest sense. Growth processes are part of life; both nourishment and growth are part of life.

And, finally, life on earth includes reproducing the whole being; the process of growth only requires that one part produce another part. Reproduction produces the whole individual being and is a higher process than mere growth.

There are no further life processes beyond these seven. Life divides into seven definite processes. But, since they serve all twelve of the sense zones, we cannot assign definite regions to these—the seven life processes enliven all the sense zones. Therefore, when we look at the way the seven relate to the twelve, we see that we have:

1. Breathing,
2. Warming,
3. Nourishing,
4. Secreting (Sorting),
5. Maintaining,
6. Growing,
7. Reproducing.

These are distinct processes, but all of them relate to each of the senses and flow through each of the senses: their relationship with the senses is a mobile one. The human being, the living human being, must be pictured as having twelve separate sense-zones through which a sevenfold life is pulsing, a mobile, sevenfold life. If you ascribe the signs of the zodiac to the twelve zones, then you have a picture of the macrocosm; if you ascribe a sense to each zone, you have the microcosm. If you assign a planet to each of the life processes, you have a picture of the macrocosm; as the life processes, they embody the microcosm. And the mobile life processes are related to the fixed zones of the senses in the same way that, in the macrocosm, the planets are related to the zones of the zodiac—they move unceasingly through them, they flow through them. And so you see in many ways the human being is a microcosm.

'Further details about the Seven Life Processes may be found in the above-mentioned lectures', writes van Houten. 'If these Seven Life Processes are not used just for the care of the body, they can be made available to the adult ego as the basis of the learning process. They can then move in two directions:

1. They can enliven our sense activity.
2. They can transform into soul forces.

Both movements are of extreme importance to the learning process, for does not every learning process move from the outside inwards (sense activity), to appear again as something 'new', after having been internalized? The direction of the first four steps of the process is from the outside in, the direction of the last three is from the inside out. The *natural* aspect of the Seven *Life* Processes is partly transformed into the *cultural* aspect of the Seven *Learning* Processes by the activity of the ego within the learning process of the adult.[45]

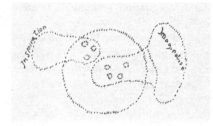

Liz's thinking now turns to the vast pictures which Steiner portrays. In Lecture eight of *The Riddle of Humanity*, Steiner describes the revivifying of the senses and draws a diagram that lines up the life processes: four planets on one side, three planets on the other side—as Liz remarks, moving towards the dynamic of the spiral of life forces in the Caduceus:

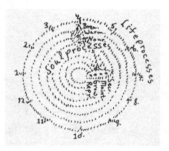

In Lecture nine, Steiner goes further to describe the ensouling of the life processes and how three new life processes arise from this ensouling: Imagination, Inspiration, Intuition:[46]

Liz's students, then, despite the material and technological distractions of our present time, experienced the right conditions to find themselves on that path of Imagination, Inspiration and Intuition which Steiner describes leading towards the realization of our full humanity—a path leading to ultimate fulfilment that he represented pictorially as the Seventh Seal, also called the Seal of the Holy Grail:[47, 48]

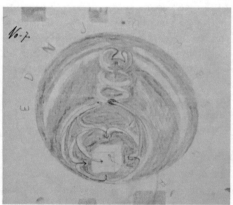

In conversation with Catherine Fenton, Liz explains the *Seal of the Holy Grail* from Steiner's presentation of it in *The Rose Cross Meditation*:

The whole picture is called the Seal of the Holy Grail and also the Seventh Seal of the Book of Revelation. Steiner says this is a picture of the human being at the end of Time, when we identify ourselves fully with the Cosmos. When we individually grow ourselves to be as big as the Cosmos. And we see it for the very first time in a completely different way: he says it was placed there as an image at the beginning of human evolution and it will be there at the end: it's the ultimate destination.

In the picture, the cube represents the physical world: a cube is a representation of space and it is transparent. The six arrows show that this cube turns

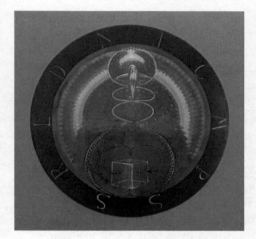

inside out. This is the inversion that I was talking about before. The snake nature has to be overcome and it transforms into the golden world spiral. The spiral meets in the transformed larynx, which becomes the Grail chalice. The dove is the Holy Spirit in the heart. So, the Holy Spirit speaks through the heart which is collected and spoken in the Grail chalice; thus we become co-creators with God. The rainbow wings are representative of human creativity—in the way the human colours their interaction with the Cosmos. Around the edge of the Seal is the Rosicrucian world motto: 'Ex Deo Nascimur' (out of God we are born); 'in Christo Morimur' (in Christ we die); and 'Per Spiritum Sanctum Reviviscimus' (through the Holy Spirit we are Resurrected).

It represents the process of becoming fully Human. So it is a massive, massive picture.

One colleague, Liz continues, 'had recognised the Caduceus as a picture of incarnating one's higher self. Which it is: it's a drop of light... Now I realised that the students are incarnating a drop of their higher self—as in the *College Imagination*, which describes moving from angels to archangels, who create a chalice. And I think the caduceus is the creation of the chalice in the individual.

'But a group can do this too: the Archangels moving between, to create the chalice, and then the Archai, who come from primal beginnings and go into infinite distances, appear only as a drop of light in this place. They are the Time spirit. So, as a College of Teachers you can incarnate a drop of Intuition that you need for the next step in your institution. You can do it on an individual learning level with your students and as an institution...'

Catherine: '...as a country...'

Liz: '...and as a world. This is the World spiral.'

A New Consciousness

In conversations through the beautiful summer of 2019, Liz shared some of the finest distillations of her thinking about intuition and truth and the path of pure thinking[49] which is, but not exclusively, 'what we do teaching literature.' It was as recent as 1939 that the term the a-ha moment was coined and its recognition is something new, like the awareness of Christ in the etheric that began around that time in the twenteth century (and also like the fairly recent coining of the word, empathy). 'This new possibility is the drop of light, given by Michael, who is the face of Christ, and it is imbued with a morality that is new. This is manifesting in the students and they know it's new. It is not coming from outside, not from their parents or teacher, it's a part of the spiritual world that is incarnating in them for the first time. And it is also an evolving part of the Christ consciousness.

'The students' experience is very often to do with Otherness and taking in the Other, with empathy and with the wider universe—somehow taking the universe with you.[50] Teaching creates a space for the imagination that can be turned into Inspiration and into this falls the drop of light: intuition. Turning imagination into Inspiration you are using the energy that's behind the imaginative process to enable the Inspiration that enables the Intuition (the moment of at-one-ment).[51]

Liz found lectures that Steiner gave over Christmas 1918-1919[52], about humankind birthing a new Christ consciousness, which are recommended reading, not least as 'the clincher' of her research. 'The task of our present age, says Steiner here, is finding the path of imagination in full consciousness. The first step has to be taken by the human being. We are not given clairvoyant visions and Imaginations by spiritual beings now, but must find our own way through the power of our human consciousness to the Spirits of Personality; to hold conversation with them as with other human beings. That is, to work as equals with angelic beings, because behind events something is trying to take place spiritually. It is not a programme, it is a reality—a social impulse linked with the impulse of freedom—which is happening as you perceive it in the moment and you have the sense of knowing it's true—my students do this,' said Liz.

Her research path not only shows us how to take the path that leads through Imagination, Inspiration and Intuition to reunion with the starry cosmos, but also the joy of those moments when we overcome the subject/object divide to find ourselves in the spirit—in unitary consciousness. Her work enables us to understand the deeper levels of those revelatory moments, those moments of epiphany, that are characteristic of every human life.

The pictures Liz has brought out of her engagement with Steiner's work are of macrocosmic proportions, but they are rooted in our everyday lives—in our relationships with each other and within ourselves. Her own journey demonstrates it. Liz discovered the path of pure thinking that Steiner offers through her daily work as a teacher of A-level Literature with young people. It is true that pure, living thinking processes are inherent to the study of literary art, but Steiner's description of reading texts in general, in the same way that Goethe read bones to discover the spiritual realities within, opens this pathway to every human being who reads textual material of any kind.[53] Everyone can use Goethean methods of observation in their own field to support their reading of 'texts as bones' or 'bones as texts' and develop their thinking along the pathway of contemplative knowledge.

Liz began her conclusions that summer by summing up Steiner's words on the significance of the Seventh Seal and its relationship to the end of time. And this led her, 'belatedly,' she writes, 'to a link with the a-ha moment that I wish I had been in a position to share earlier. Here are Steiner's full words, which are some of the most far reaching he ever pronounced. Having talked about the movement of the Sun and the Planets in the 'world spiral' he adds:

> You can see here what significance the spiral has for the bodies of the universe; and these bodies represent a figure with which the human being will eventually be identified. When that time comes human beings will have purified their productive powers; the larynx will then be the organ of reproduction. That which the human being will have developed as the purified body of the snake will then no longer work from below upwards but from above downwards. The transformed larynx in us will become the chalice which we call the Holy Grail. And just as the one is purified, so will the other be purified, that other which is combined with this reproductive organ. It will be an essence of the universal power, the great universal essence. And this universal spirit is depicted in its essence in the image of the dove confronting the Holy Grail face to face. This is the symbol of that spiritualised impregnation which will work from out of the cosmos when the human being has become identified with the cosmos. The creative element of this process is depicted in the rainbow: this is the all-embracing seal of the Holy Grail.[54]

'Suddenly the significance of the words "when the human being has become identified with the cosmos" were borne in upon me. In *every* a-ha moment there is an overcoming, sometimes greater, sometimes lesser, of the object/subject divide. This is a moment where, in our small corner of the world, each of us identifies with a part of the cosmos that we have not "perceived" before. Every time this happens in an individual each Aha/ Epiphany/Revelation/Eureka moment becomes a step towards Homo sapiens *realising* our ultimate destiny. It is a step towards "knowing" the cosmos, and therefore loving it, enabling our will to act in accordance with the 'willing of the Spirit."[55]

In the 'absolute conclusion' to her research work, Liz returned to Steiner's 'diagram of the Seventh Seal as a picture of the human being at the end of time, when the whole human being is identified with the cosmos and we will grow to the size of the cosmos in order to become one with the cosmos.' Here she reiterates, 'We will know the cosmos and love the cosmos and become co-creative with the cosmos. Every time a human being has a moment of epiphany, part of them identifies with a part of the cosmos and, in taking a step towards that ultimate revelation, they take the rest of humanity with them as a deed.

'We are Homo *sapiens*—our task is to know—to know is to love and to love is to know—and thus we become co-creators in the cosmos.'[56]

PART TWO: A PRACTICAL GUIDE

CULTIVATING THE CONDITIONS FOR A-HA MOMENTS AND LIVING THINKING IN THE CLASSROOM

Catherine Fenton's guide to applying Liz Attwell's pioneering work in educational practice

Liz and I started to plan a booklet of her teaching ideas soon after she first became ill. I was fortunate enough to spend several happy and inspiring years observing her extraordinary lessons, and planning lessons and co-teaching with her. I saw students who were actively engaged in their learning and thinking whilst also having enormous fun—surely the 'holy grail' for each teacher! It felt important to capture as many of her lessons and ideas as we could when it became clear that she would not be able to go into teacher training and share her ideas widely in person.

Soon we realized that we could break down her classroom approach into ten different steps that build upon each other but do not need to be followed as a linear process. You may find the early steps are much in use with the start of a new group or course, gradually allowing you to move towards the latter stages with a class, or you may use each step, or only one or two, in every lesson. I have had many wonderful moments in the classroom using Liz's ideas and techniques for active learning—I hope you do too.

— *Catherine Fenton*

1. Humour, Fun and Silliness

When a teacher takes a new class of adolescents for the first time, they are often faced by a multitude of attitudes: bolshiness, raw self-consciousness, enthusiasm, fear of looking stupid, habitual laziness, expectations of boredom, love for learning, academic precociousness, brittle intellectual pretension to name but a few.

Our favourite way of subverting these expectations, breaking down barricades, and uniting the class in the hopeful feeling that this might be quite fun after all, is to start off with very silly games. With icebreakers— laughter-inducing games with physical contact, finding ways for them to forget their awkward adolescent selves briefly and to enjoy each other's company—you can start to build relationships based on truth and trust not protective facades. You are subverting their expectations of the class solely involving hard slog on serious, dry essays or tests, and showing that humour and energy will be involved in their learning too.

At this stage, although we take themes from whatever text we are studying or are about to study—there is no overt emphasis on too much learning from the game, rather fun, warm ups that loosen up the students, relax them, and start to set them in the atmosphere or world of the text and allow them to experience this from different perspectives. We often took Bothmer gym children's games or Forest school activities, and made simple adjustments in theme.

Examples of this in practice

Life of Pi
Students had to cross the room from the 'boat' to the safe 'raft' without being caught by a 'shark,' in the style of 'stick in the mud,' a childrens' game.

Becoming a shark
Pair off and play rock, paper, scissors. The loser then holds onto the back of the winner's shoulders and they find another pair to play, making the 'shark' bigger each time. Eventually the whole class will be united behind one final winner.

Karmic knot exercise
The students all stand in a circle with their eyes closed and arms out in front, walking slowly forwards until they can find two other hands to grasp. They then untangle the giant knot they have created, without dropping hands.

Making machines together
Give the students four minutes in groups to create, for example, a moving steam train or clock (i.e. when introducing the Industrial Revolution), with their bodies. For example, four people become carriages by linking arms, then other students enact the wheels beside them, chimneys, drivers etc. can be added and a lot of noise created to create the atmosphere of the train.
This immediately puts students in a place of creativity and collaborative thinking and can be applied to any subject with a little imagination, usually generating a great deal of laughter and discussion.

Nutty Squirrels
Pair off the students. One becomes the mother and one becomes the baby (or master/ servant, for example, if this is a theme in the text).
The baby is blindfolded and neither can talk. Each pair must work out

a system of communication whereby the mother can guide the baby to 'nuts' (folded socks) when you begin the game—and then help them to aim the socks to knock out other couples from the game. If a baby is hit the pair are out, if the mother is hit the baby goes it alone (still blindfolded), while everyone who is out watches in silent hilarity from the edges. The last pair or baby left in wins. For such a fun game there can be an enormous amount of learning on various levels and themes—which you may choose to draw out afterwards.

2. Movement

Sitting in a hard chair for a whole lesson is no fun for anyone, and can be a form of torture for many students, as well as seriously bad for everyones' health. If they are allowed to move part of the time, they must stay awake, their circulation keeps moving well, and their thinking will be brighter and more engaged (make sure you plan in the same for yourself as a teacher). Building on the fun and silliness of Step 1, moving around with games and exercises allows students to experience the subject they are learning, to step into a place or a character's experience, whether that of Churchill, a Roman emperor or Atticus Finch.

In addition, using the physical body in space and time makes opportunities for new connections and frees up the intellect from calcified, 2D learning. Keeping the hand and heart as well as the head engaged in learning in teenage years allows flexible, healthy, embodied learning. When your body interacts with other bodies, perceptions can change, new ideas can enter and the subject or topic becomes enlivened and embodied.

Examples of this in practice

To Kill A Mockingbird
The students were randomly given a red, blue or yellow badge and asked to circulate around a stage following certain rules. The red badges acknowledged no one but each other, the blue badges bowed to the red badges but ignored the yellow, and the yellow badges had to bow to everyone.

Liz observed that within a few minutes, this extremely simple exercise nearly led to outbreaks of violence. The conversation afterwards about what everyone had experienced led to far deeper levels of discussion than merely teaching the textual context of unequal and racist societies.

Dulce et Decorum Est

To introduce World War One poetry, Catherine had the whole class climb into a ditch in front of our school building. When she blew a whistle, everyone had to climb out and walk slowly into a line towards the other 'trench', and two fairly accurate 'machine gunners' who 'shot' people down. Two randomly allocated generals were allowed to stay and shout encouragement from the trench, and the winners were any who reached the other side safely. Of course there were no winners, apart from the generals, and soon Catherine was under attack herself by students who said that the game was 'rigged', 'impossible', 'unfair' and needed rule changes or it wouldn't work, and also had she considered that this game was disrespectful to those who had died in the trenches AND she should have given a trigger warning at the beginning of the game. Then everyone went upstairs in the perfect mood to start reading Wilfred Owen's World War One poetry.

Of Mice and Men

One student had to lead a blindfolded student around, keeping them safe and telling them exactly what to do next. They quickly tired both of the responsibility of leading, and the helplessness of following, thus echoing some of the experiences of the two protagonists in *Of Mice and Men*, and leading to empathy with the ruler as well as the follower.

3. Raising the Text from the Page in Imaginative Ways or Bringing the Phenomena to Life

Building on the principles of fun and movement, it also seems unfair to ask students to sit still and read out or listen to texts which were designed to be leapt, shouted and tip-toed across a stage—with props! Reading the black and white text of a play is only looking at the skeleton of the thing, the fossilized remains of a living, breathing event.

Shakespeare is often the most complex and oldest writing that students will encounter and as it was written for lively, colourful performance it simply cannot be studied effectively as a dead piece of text, just as a song needs to be sung not just read.

Most teachers know this already because it's obvious that plays and songs must be performed to be fully understood, but what about poems, essays and novels? And what about in other subjects, how can we start to raise them from the textbooks to becoming living, meaningful phenomena?

Everything can be improved by being brought to life, especially with students who do not read fluidly and may need help to visualize the action, scene, scientific phenomenon or historical event.

Small group-work on scenes, playing together with where to stand, what to wear and how to act each character, allows learning both in rehearsal and then in the performance to other students. Acting out the plot of an entire novel in 60 seconds allows new patterns or ideas to emerge—whilst, of course, allowing the revision of plot in a lively and engaged way.

Putting a poem, scene or chapter into a contemporary or different context, with props, can completely transform a reading of it, highlighting or pulling out new interpretations and showing how the text can be understood, and therefore its continued importance, in the light of today's issues.

In other subjects, the same principles can be applied. Historical scenes can be acted out, with everyone playing a battleship, a fighter pilot or a politician as necessary. Scientific phenomena need to be practically explored and enacted, not taught by rote (as Steiner made so very clear when describing how to teach Lower School science). The traditional example might be acting out the movement and placement of the planets on the playing field, or perhaps the artistic depiction of the gases on a planet, and beginning science blocks with practical experiments such as looking at torchlight through cloudy water and observing the colours.

Examples of this in practice

Pride and Prejudice
Two students performed Darcy and Elizabeth's famous dance and verbal sparring match, but set at a disco, translated into modern teen speech.

The Comedy of Errors
Split the Prologue into four lines for each group to act out. Visually establishing what happened and the order of events, showing how bizarre they are, and starting to draw out themes of the entire play.

Angela Carter's Wise Children
We recreated the scene of the wild party at the end, with pretend snogging behind the blackboard, someone banging the walls and someone else shaking the lights, to bring to life the bacchanal Carter conjures up.

Macbeth
Each table had to re-enact the witches' first speech as different groups of modern stereotypes. Coffee morning mums, high speed bankers, politicians, football hooligans... not only was every interpretation

very funny, it also allowed the students to grapple with the meaning of every line and then try to apply the meaning to a very new situation, leading to thorough understanding and very fruitful analysis of the speech afterwards.

Articles
When faced with contrasting the tone of two different articles, we split the group in half and they acted out one article each, with props. When one article ended up with students 'giving birth' on tables and prancing around the room joyfully enacting modern cosmic metaphors and the other ended with the narrator weeping into her handkerchief, the contrast became obvious and many points raised for the ensuing written work.

Geography
'You are a farmer, you are a Monsanto executive, you are an NGO, act out this scenario...'

'Believe me, everything we mediate to the children via feelings allows their inner life to grow, while an education that consists of mere thoughts and ideas is devoid of life, remains dead.'
    Steiner, *Education for Adolescents*

4. Colourful and Expansive Resources

If you oblige students to study lines of small black print and unattractive resources, and then have them write only in biro on narrowly lined paper, on a daily basis, you cramp their imagination and confine their thinking to the straight and narrow. Of course, an essay must be written in this way (or must it?!), but in all the stages of analysis, discussion, and planning, we think you should go big, colourful and free. Big mind maps, diagrams and drawings allow creative thinking, freedom of interpretation and new connections between issues as you open up the text or subject.

Don't demand immaculate presentation every day—allow for different styles of planning and thinking.

Examples of this in practice

Get rid of: Lined A4 paper and black biros.
Use: Big pieces of paper, lots of colourful sharpies and crayons, sticky labels, other resources like playdough, fabric scraps, paint, any other medium possible.
Get the students to make: Set designs, mind maps, structures, charts, maps, cartoons/comic strips, mood boards, word definitions. Put these

resources on the wall and refer to them again and again. Once you get into the habit of trying out these different formats, lessons basically plan themselves, and students may start skipping into your classes, enthused about trying out a new skill.

For homework, ask your students to create a big magazine collage of the setting of a play or novel, or of how they imagine a character. They may end up setting *Twelfth Night* in a two-storey gay club or in corporate London—genius!—which opens up so many new avenues to explore in subsequent discussions.

Do sculptures of scientific concepts and write mathematical equations for poetry. Make land art in language lessons and foreign menus in cooking class! Cross-pollinate and try to use attractive, colourful resources to engage the imagination and open up horizons.

5. Bringing Together Unexpected Things to See What Emerges

Like a good metaphor, bringing new, apparently unconnected things together can spark off a whole new world of ideas.

Putting old plays into new settings is the classic way of doing this, and can be incredibly fun and fruitful for the students. This allows them to relate to characters and bring them to life, finding new angles and connections within the play.

Comparing two texts allows one to reveal itself anew in comparison with the other, the similarities and differences allow both to resonate as you turn your gaze from one to the other, whilst holding both in your consciousness.

Finding new angles of enquiry is a classic approach to having that a-ha moment, in literature, science, or other areas.

Examples of this in practice

A Midsummer Night's Dream
In groups, create a new setting for the play.
One group of students set the play on different planets—mechanicals, Greeks etc. all had their own planet, with bridges to cross over, forest planet.
Another group set it on the underground, circle line, every station was a different world.
Yet another set it in the Shard with bankers.
Or at their school—the maintenance team were the mechanicals, etc.

Each group managed to discover totally different interpretations and ideas about the play with their new settings.

The Charge of the Light Brigade and Dulce at Decorum Est
The students acted out one of the poems in a group, then Catherine asked them to create a mash up with the other group so that the contrast between the two poets' voices became amplified in a very dramatic way. Suddenly the two differing perspectives on war became achingly clear as the glorious cavalry charge was overlaid with the sound of men dying from a gas attack, spiralling together to a brutal crescendo.

Other examples are re-writing a fairy tale in modern life, à la Angela Carter, or mix and matching fairy tales with other genres and re-writing the story in that style.

Catherine has just had some students rehearse and re-enact Sonnet 116 as a brilliant modern day rap with great success, leading to a much deeper understanding of the poem itself.

Business Studies
Write a new business model for Coca Cola, based entirely on sustainability.

Redesign the marketing for a certain type of car to appeal to a new consumer group.

Geography or History
Join the dots between different phenomena or features throughout the ages. Work on cross-curricular projects with different teachers and see what emerges or evolves.

6. Learning to Pay Attention to the Phenomena

Once your students are relaxed and eager to learn, comfortable in the class and with each other, with the creative juices flowing—the real work begins! It's most important that students have an experience of the actual phenomena they are studying, not just information about it. As Liz says, 'Pure observation is key, structure explains everything, and the medium itself is the message.'

Information kills learning, so begin with primary phenomena and never lead with context. Ensure that the students have the experience first—in English the text itself (resurrected in activities as it has died in print) before bringing in anything else. All of the steps mentioned previously are also working on this principle—every time they act out a scene in different accents or moods, draw out the structure of a chapter or a whole poem, write about a character: they are learning the text inside out and upside down and beginning to really know it. At this point, they can begin to see patterns, draw together different parts of the text, and to see it as a whole.

It's important to train teenagers out of a superficial and floppy response of sympathy and antipathy, i.e. their likes or dislikes. It doesn't immediately matter whether a text or painting is good or bad, what IS it?

What is it doing?
How is it doing it?
Why is it doing it?

Teenagers can have a tendency to spill out their feelings, likes or dislikes, but if they can learn to withhold judgement and just wait, they can store and build up energy to spiral upwards into new insight.

Goethean Science—a reminder

Observe exactly, without bringing preconceptions to the observations.
Bring the phenomenon into active relationship with each other.
Listen inwardly to perceive 'dawning realizations.'
Act on intuitions.

Examples of this in practice

Socratic questioning of a text: generate three questions each and listen to everyone's questions, then generate more. Do not answer the questions, but allow them to spark more and more.
Draw up the structure of the text, beginning , middle and end.
Give groups of students small parts of the whole to analyse in depth and then each group presents their findings in order.
Art is also an ideal subject for pure observation, in other subjects you need to work harder to give students this experience. In maths, for example, students need to go through the whole process manually, and understand what they are doing, before being taught any short cuts to a calculation. Waldorf Lower school science is excellent at this—students observe simple experiments—phenomena first—and only afterwards start to conceptualize the experience and draw conclusions. Steiner said that teaching like this ensures that you are giving students living concepts to work with throughout their lifetime, not injecting them with dead and fossilized ideas.
History can be more difficult as naturally you are often dealing with secondary sources. Teachers look for primary sources wherever possible: films, original documents and photographs, listen to speeches, observe clothes and tools from the age. In Geography, they look at a cliff or a

stone or a river and observe clearly, perhaps sketching or discussing, but not applying too much theory at the beginning.

Catherine had a lot of fun as a student teacher with David Smith's excellent and intelligent class. Asked to teach statistics and graphs, she set up the class in groups to survey the entire school on subjects that interested them, such as musical instruments played or which month people were born in. The class spent a fun and engaged morning questioning students from every year group, and then put together their results in various graphs. In their subsequent presentations we learnt some genuinely interesting patterns, such as more males than females being born in certain seasons of the year. It was a simple and interactive way to understand the point of statistics and graphs.

'Goethe's method can be adapted for use in the classroom. The first step is to apply rigorous observation of the phenomenon. This differs from conventional science which tends to form a hypothesis and then test it through experiment, often by separating the phenomenon into its constituent parts and analysing them. Goethe laid a strong emphasis on studying the phenomena in context. With the plant this takes the form of studying it where it grows, over a long period of time, and really coming to know the plants form and structure. In literature this is analogous to the stage at which we are reading the text, simply establishing exactly what is going on, and then moving to a comprehensive understanding of its constituent parts within the form and structure.'
Liz Attwell, 'Riding the Magic Carpet'

7. Bin the Experts and Toss out the Textbooks: Students Create Their Own Learning Resources and Opinions

'Migraine-like conditions are the result of a one-sided stuffing of material that must be learned without pleasure. The children are then filled with tiny spikes that do not get dissolved. They tend toward developing such spikes. Yes—we must be aware of these problems.'
Steiner, *Education for Adolescents*

There are times when students do need to memorize information that other people have worked out and written down for them but this should not be where learning begins, or ends.

'but do you know, we never ask questions, or at least most don't; they just run the answers at you, bing, bing, bing, and us sitting there for four more hours of film-teacher. That's not social to me at all. It's a lot of funnels and lot of water poured down the spout and out the bottom, and them telling us it's wine when it's not.' Ray Bradbury, *Fahrenheit 451*.

When students are simply given a textbook or lecture of other people's facts, perceptions and opinions to work through and learn, they are effectively being told that their thoughts or insights into the subject being studied are unimportant. Imagine the end result of a whole school career like this.

This ties in entirely with the key step of observation. Students cannot observe clearly if they are desperately trying to remember what they read in the textbook, or scrabbling for a half-remembered context. Throw out the expert opinions until the students have formed their own, there will be a time and a place to bring in quotes and context to back up their well-thought out opinions. Give them the 'mantle of the expert' (Dorothy Heathcote).

'If we spend too much time pouring a mass of information over young people at this age, or if we teach in such a way that they never come to lift their doubts and questions into consciousness, then, even though we are the more objective party, we expose, even if indirectly, our latent inadequacies.'
Steiner, *Education for Adolescents*

Examples of this in practice

Instead of asking students to read a professor's opinion of what they should see in a poem, have them analyse a poem in groups and create a large diagram about it on poster paper. Give them the right questions or areas to work on, and teach them the names of techniques they might not yet know. As they dissect the poem, throw in new questions if needed.

Have the group teach the rest of the class what they have discovered, with their poster elaborating and illustrating all of their points. The class can ask questions afterwards which may provide further illumination. Restrain your ego—everyone already knows you are an expert in this subject.

Make the students the experts! Call an examiners' meeting and assign them all the task of creating next year's exam questions. Through the process of examining what the exam needs to demand of students; and which questions would work to pull out certain elements of each text; and how to word each question to support the students to achieve success in their responses—they can learn so much about exam technique, from a position of power and creativity.

'The second step is "exact sensory perception." As Goethe puts it "we initially see the different leaves as discrete steps in a process," however, he says that to understand the growth of the plant, an intrinsic unity, we have to think the growth sequences through time (Goethe did it both forwards and backwards). Each leaf or part of the plant becomes a snapshot in time of a continuous process. When he did this Goethe experienced, as Miller put it, "the dynamic inward archetype" or as Goethe put it, the Urphenomenon. In my study of literature I lay great emphasis on the structure of the text. The scenes of a play, chapters of a book, or the verses of a poem can be seen as analogous to the leaves on the plant.'
Liz Attwell, 'Riding the Magic Carpet'

8. Demand Independent Thought by Asking the Right Questions

And more importantly, by showing students how to formulate their own questions. This is already implicit in the activities described thus far. Reducing teacher talking time as the main learning method of a class does not reduce the importance of the work of a teacher. In asking the right questions and guiding the work of each student, and bringing in facts and engaging context at the correct time, you lead them helpfully in their own research and discoveries in a way that inspires their love of learning and asking their own questions of the world, instead of deadening their interest by prescribing answers and opinions. Teaching students to observe properly and ask original questions requires more confidence than lecturing with proficiency on a subject you know well, and it requires more preparation, including practice at forming open-ended questions (Shirley Clarke's Formative Assessment is an excellent place to look at this skill).

Examples

What questions can we ask…?

Can we draw the structure of this?

What do we see…?

As a group, can you find a pattern in this…?

In pairs, come up with five possible reasons for…?

What comparisons can we make between this and this? What do the similarities and differences show us?

How can you test this idea?

'When we do not have enough interest in the world around us, then we are thrown back into ourselves. Taken all in all, we have to say that if we look at the chief damages created by modern civilization, they arise primarily because people are far too concerned with themselves and do not usually spend the larger part of their leisure time in concern for the world but busy themselves with how they feel and what gives them pain... And the least favourable time of life to be self-occupied in this way is during the ages between fourteen, fifteen, and twenty-one years old.'

Steiner, *Education for Adolescents*

9. Lift off- Riding the Magic Carpet Together

The most significant aspect of many of these ten steps is bringing together a class to work imaginatively and respectfully. Through drama, movement, laughter, many hours spent sharing sharpies over posters and mind maps, and the respectful attitude of the teacher towards everyone's contributions: a community of truly supportive learning can be built. The students treasure this long after the lessons have ended.

This atmosphere is important because it frees up everyone to trust that their ideas or insights, however 'wacky', will be received thoughtfully and evaluated with consideration, allowing them to take risks with their thinking and make imaginative leaps that may lead to new insight.

When a student group who know and trust each other, with common experiences but also different personalities and skills, think creatively and collaboratively on a problem, all sorts of previously unturned material and knowledge can be pulled into play by the interactions between them.

And sometimes a student will state a question or thought that sets a whole class in motion, building a new picture or interpretation together that can take them to a totally original perception.

Ideas on how to set up the optimal learning environment

Seminar style classroom setup—either one long table that everyone can sit around, or several groups sat around tables together. No lines of desks facing the teacher at the front. Teacher not at head of table either! The teacher always models thoughtful, courteous, enthusiastic and supportive behaviour.

Consciously work on group bonds from the very start and cultivate a strong sense of identity as a class. Have lots of paired discussions and

group activities, making sure that students get a chance to work closely
with everyone else in the class.
Always identify 'mistakes' in a gentle way and move on quickly, so that
students trust your judgement but feel safe to take risks anyway.
Be excited about discovering new things!

10. A-ha!

Your eyes might light up, or your mouth opens, you look up, throw your
hands in the air, you start to shake, perhaps you jump out of the bath and
run down the street naked...

Whatever you do when a fresh and true new insight hits you, or dawns
upon you, or strikes you, everyone knows how it feels to have that a-ha
moment. 'Eureka!', a light bulb above your head, that flash when a previously unclear picture opens up to reveal a solution that you know is true.
Think of the happy moment you solve a riddle after approaching it from
every possible angle, the pieces falling into place to create a cohesive
answer.

Liz described it recently as the moment that a 'ragged and colourful
kaleidoscope turns into a beautiful mandala in the backspace of your
thinking.' This clarity can come to an individual or a group.

Showing students how to reach these moments of insight purpose-
fully themselves gives them the ability to see things truly by looking and
thinking for themselves; knowing when they have had a real insight by
the process they have gone through. Guiding students to ask real questions, look at the actual phenomena and build upwards instead of going
straight for a quick and easy solution as served up by someone else (for
example a politician or the media) gives them a freedom and a questioning confidence that will allow them to develop into the type of adult that
our society so urgently needs.

PART THREE: THE DIARY

My diary is the document in which I recorded the process I went through as I researched. I have not changed one word from this document, except to protect identities, and when I have expanded a reference so that, if you are interested, you can look it up. There are intimate personal details included, though not many, which I would ask you to treat with respect. I left these in because I wanted to reflect the way that a teacher's ordinary mundane existence can be intertwined with the superconscious.

At Christmas 2010 my Secret Santa from college gave me a beautiful unlined notebook in bright pink leather. I felt it deserving of something special. I put it in my bedside drawer and resolved to try to keep a diary. Many people had mentioned the value of this, but I had always quickly grown bored with the practice. Sure enough I made ten entries between 1 March and 2 April 2011 before it tailed off! My next entry, 27 September 2012, a good 18 months later, shows a big jump in engagement.

One sees me, tentatively at first, jump from the secondary consciousness in the first entries, to an intense working with the phenomena that I and my pupils are experiencing. My work on the phenomena start to take on the character of being 'imbued with imagination'—the first step in the 'new clairvoyance' that Rudolf Steiner describes. Then you begin to see answers coming back, in the form of inspirations from the spirits of personality, which forms the second step in the new clairvoyance. There are even flashes of 'a drop of light, bestowed by the ruling spirit of our age'—Intuition.

From *Supersensible Man, Freewill and the Immortality of the Soul*. May 1, 1918. Out of *Rudolf Steiner on his book Philosophy of Freedom* edited by Otto Palmer:

> Twenty-five years ago (in *Philosophy of Freedom*), I applied the term 'intuitive thinking' to what I am now describing as an attribute of pure thinking born of intuition and making its appearance in moral rather than in logical concepts when a person acts in accordance with moral ideas... When one becomes aware that an unconscious inspiration lives at one pole of their being and an unconscious imagination at the other, s/he becomes aware of an immortal part. Though in ordinary life this awareness remains at an unconscious or subconscious level, it is nevertheless present. It is present in unconscious inspirations, as also in moral ideas, regardless of whether they are right or wrong; it is present on occasions

when we are not taken up with ourselves, but develop—in warmth of love for an action such as I described—an energy that carries us beyond the confines of self-interest.

Here something remarkable reveals itself in human nature. When something that is otherwise present only at an unconscious level, namely, this unconscious imagination that is a personal possession and that, as I described, can only be made effective by love, works in concert with intuitive or inspired thinking as this shines in from its own sphere to illumine ideas…when this thinking, that is born not of man's immortal part but of what is immortal in him/her, works in concert with the imagination that ordinarily remains unconscious but takes on an instinctual character in us when we conceive love for an action… when, as I say, this instinctive love, which is an instinctual expression of the imagination described, acts on a person in such a way as to move him/her to make use through inspiration of what shines into her/him from the time before her birth, then an immortal element works on the immortal element in the human being. An idea, born of the immortal world that we experience before our birth, works in concert with the immortal element that manifests itself on an unconscious level in imagination and returns again to the spiritual world through the gates of death.

Thus the human being is capable of actions in which his immortal part, otherwise revealed only after death, becomes an effective force during his earthly life and works in concert with free ideas issuing, through inspiration, from the immortal realm in the form of impulses that enter our human personalities before birth. This is then *free* deed.

This freedom of action is a human potentiality, and man is aware of possessing it. One learns to understand what freedom is only when one knows that unconscious imagination, which builds toward our life after death, works in concert with unconscious inspiration, the latter a force emanating from our life before birth and playing into our souls. …Mortal man is en route to freedom. As mortal man goes on making the immortal man in him ever more conscious, s/he becomes aware of her/his freedom. The human being is born to freedom, *but s/he must educate herself to realise it.*

The diary moves from a realization of the process of judgement to a moment where I solemnly declare that I am in the Presence of the Holy Grail—23 December 2012.

A significant moment happens on 4 November in which I draw my first diagram of my experience of an a-ha moment.

Last night reading to prepare for death, I came across the clearest corroboration from Steiner I have ever found! I will quote it now:

From *Staying Connected: How to continue your relationships with those who have died*, pp 98-100. Taken from Rudolf Steiner's lecture 'The Blessings of the Dead,' Paris, 26 May 1914.

As we liberate our thinking from the body, we feel as though our thinking has been snatched away from us, as though it has expanded and spread out in space and time. Thinking, which we normally say takes place inside us, unites with the surrounding spiritual world, streams into it, and achieves a certain autonomy from us similar to the relative independence of the eyes, which are set in their sockets rather like autonomous organs. Thus, although our liberated thinking is connected with our higher self, it is independent enough to act as our spiritual organ of perception for the thoughts and feelings of other spiritual beings. Its function is thus similar to that of our eyes. Gradually, the thinking processes, normally limited by our intelligence, becomes independent from our being as spiritual organs of perception.

To put it differently, what we experience subjectively, what is comprised by our intelligence, namely our outer thinking, is nothing but shadowy entities, thought entities, mere ideas reflecting external things. When thinking becomes clairvoyant and separates from the brain and nervous system, it begins to develop inner activity, a life of its own, and to stream out, as our own experience, into the spiritual world. In a sense, we send the tendrils of our clairvoyant thinking out into the spiritual realm and, as they become immersed in this world, they perceive the willing that feels and feeling that wills of the other beings in that realm.

After what we have said about self-knowledge being a necessity on the path of spiritual development—and from this it follows that modesty is a must—allow me to comment on clairvoyant thinking; please do not think me presumptuous for saying this. When we enliven our thinking through clairvoyant development, it becomes independent and also a very precise and useful tool. True clairvoyance increases the precision, accuracy and logical power of our thinking. As a result, we can use it with more exactness and closer adaption to its subject; our intelligence becomes more practical and more thoroughly structured. Therefore, the clairvoyant can easily understand the scope of ordinary scientific research, whereas conventional science requires bringing out ... of the mind. It is easy to see why modern natural science cannot comprehend the findings of clairvoyant research, while those who have developed true clairvoyance can comprehend the full significance of the achievements of the natural sciences. There can be no question, therefore, of spiritual science opposing conventional science; the other way around is more likely. Only clairvoyant development can organise the power of the mind, making it inwardly independent, alive, comprehensible. That is why the materialistic way of thinking cannot penetrate to the logic that gives us the certainty that clairvoyant knowledge really does lead to perception of the spiritual world. [.....]

As specifically human qualities, intellect and thinking can be developed only in human beings on earth, and they allow even people who are not clairvoyant to understand the results of clairvoyant research. You see, our independent thinking becomes the spiritual eye, as it were, for the perception of the spiritual world. Supersensible research, which uses this spiritual eye for clairvoyant thinking, has found that this eye is active, that the spiritual feelers are put out in all directions, but our physical eyes only passively allow impressions to come to them. When we as spiritual researchers have taken the revelations of the supersensible world into our thinking, they continue to live in our thoughts. We can then tell other people about what we have taken pains to bring into our living thought processes, and they can understand us if they do not allow materialistic prejudices to get in the way.

Elizabeth Barrett Attwell's Diary

Tues. 1st March 2011

My first attempt. I assume I will get better at it. My child and I worked amicably over supper—an achievement on both sides. Shopped for food—quite the provider.

Must ring a pupil's parents to explain that he must work on his essay.

Walked—which was good.

Trouble waking up—2 bad nights.

Wed. 2nd March

Beaux Stratagem (the Class 12 play) is a triumph. Cooked sausage and mash. My daughter baby sat. Need to contact a colleague. Lunch with another colleague—she is full of future plans—wants to work with Jane. Tried to get my child to take monetary responsibility!

Thurs. 3rd March

Won twice at cards. Special roast smoked salmon for supper. No lessons to teach today, but put in exam entries. Had a good rest. Spoke to staffing and said that I would take 18 lessons next year. Had a crisis this morning and felt like jacking it all in. Talked to Nic and felt better. Walked.

Mon. 7th March

Watched the news—Libya descending into civil war. Read *Lord of the Rings* to my son. Ham and fried potato for supper. Taught AS. They are not so impressed with *Small Island*. Enjoying looking forward to *Frankenstein*.

Made a pupil cry about her homework. Was outspoken about the whole group.

My son getting ready to be an England fan for carnival.

Tues. 8th March

My child got an offer of a place at Canterbury. Went to Pizza Express to celebrate.

Carnival—dressed as Macbeth. Jane—Lady Macbeth.

Talked to the gym teacher about Bothmer and contacting the dead and seeing Apotheosis! He was open.

Symbolism in *Small Island* for the AS.

My son an English supporter.

Wed. 9th March

AGM—low key. The chairman of governors challenged me to get important speakers. School lost £150,000 last year.

My child happy because she got a place at Canterbury.

A.S. enjoyed looking at scenes from *Beaux Stratagem*—

Beautiful walk—my aunt died, must write to my uncle.

Thurs. 10th March

Mum's death day. 12 years.

Must write to my uncle.

Fish and chip supper.

U.S. Meeting—lively study based on the teenage edge—I told of my experiences of the etheric heart—others contributed but not the same precision. Everyone really engaged with the book however.

Wed. 16th March

I have missed 6 days. Vital things that have happened…

Bothmer gym—revitalizing.

On Monday a pupil was telling me she wants to act and I realised that rather than teach her English I should be helping her to *speak* with her full voice. I am trying to live with that thought.

Felt ill—period—flattening.

Tues. 22nd March

Talked on the phone to a colleague—she is machinating.

Saw a friend—who is beautiful but much more frail.

A beautiful day.

Nic is ill and on antibiotics.

Sat 2nd April 2011

Really suffering from a blocked eustachian tube and incipient ear infection. Really tried to relax and look after myself. Hope it is working. I am quite scared.

My daughter involved with my son's chickens and made me breakfast. What a difference for me.

27th September 2012

Big jump—I enjoyed reading 18 months ago—it seems longer.

Had an extraordinary summer.—Stopped menstruating a year ago! I am sure that as the womb withers other capacities are born.

So am trying to write down all my insights—I thought I could try here.

Realised etheric heart.

In summer inset day described how thinking is taken down through the heart and inverts and comes back up—to inspired thought outside the head.—Lights up the constellations of stars which dimmed to make the etheric heart.

Then found Steiner's diagram in *The Human Soul in Relation to the World Evolution*!!! Says that thoughts are warmed by urges, desires, instincts, forces—purified to achieve imagination and inspiration. Also Steiner's diagram of the eye shows relationship of picture forming stream (10% astral?) to experience stream (90% etheric?). Memories are the etheric stream *recalled up*.

—Could Dyslexia be a change in the relationship between Astral and Etheric.—Etheric becomes more dominant?—Disrupts Astral?

Mon 1st Oct 2012

In *New View* Jeremy Naydler is writing about Google glasses which will 'overlay' our sight with information from the internet. Technology tends to display outwardly characteristics of what we [need] capacities which are becoming available to us. Therefore, perhaps it is becoming possible for us to experience this activity of the 'overlay' concept analogous to the activity of the overlaying of the complementary colour in a more direct way than heretofore.

'Augmented reality' glasses. 'The virtual context is directly and compellingly overlaid onto the real.'

'The challenge of addressing the hunger that humanity feels so strongly for greater connection with the realm of the spirit, and which many mistakenly seek to satisfy through greater connection to technology.'

'Now seems like a good time to attend to the opening of the inner eye.' Richard Bunzl.

'When confronted by an object that you are able to think about you come into touch with the entire entelechy, the entire existence. It is an intuition of the wholeness of an object.'

'We have the possibility of knowing it (any object) in its fullness.'—Steiner *Philosophy of Freedom*

'By thinking we fit together again into one piece all that we have taken apart through perceiving.' (p. 74)

'Cultivating on sense of life is one way we can do this.' (Bunzl)

2nd Oct 2012

Steiner's lecture on the eye

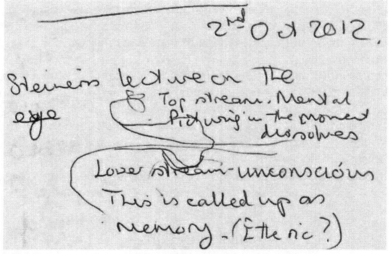

Michaela, the Eurythmy teacher commented,—this is why you know something when you have done it (!).

How is this related to the birth of the etheric? Stream is one (?) when younger—separates when you begin to say 'I.' (!?)

3rd Oct

Is a new capacity being born? Shown outwardly by the development of internet information overlaying our perceptions of the world. A fuller reflection of a new ability to tune into the inner etheric activity of the soul.

Sherlock showed this on TV—lots of people loved it. Billiard player in Ken Robinson's *The Element* saw geometrical lines on the table.

7th Oct

We could build a new curriculum on Goethean observation—(achieving flow!) that would be truly creative. *How* to be creative *and* scientific. The 'Rational' and the 'Natural' according to Ken Robinson.

Thought: read 'What Coleridge Knew'!!

8th Oct

Our organs can become sense-organs. As the etheric loosens and the astral can enter (?)—this is the extra 90%.

Dad's Death Day—14 years.

Recall is designed to put us in touch with the 90%. The Rückshau builds a connection to the 90%.

5 values I stand for (an attempt)

- Kindness
- Loyalty
- Truth
- Honour
- Beauty

13th Oct

Susanne Fuller pointed out that we give unfinished toys to small children to call forth this etheric activity. And we massage for a short time to allow the body/etheric to finish the job.

Complementary Colours and The Act of Cognition: An Open Secret

(Some thoughts in response to Diana Pauli's demonstration on *A Goethean Approach to Colour as a Pathway to the Spirit*)

There has always been a fascination, especially in Anthroposophical circles, with the phenomenon of the eye's production of a complementary colour in response to the act of concentrating on a colour on a white background: blue and yellow, magenta and green etc. There has been a feeling that somehow this has significance but it has been unclear, at least to me, as to exactly why. In his course on light in 1919 Steiner suggested that the etheric is 'looser' in the eye than in the rest of the body and that through observing its action we might be able to study the etheric.

According to Diana Pauli the complementary colour is composed of the wavelengths that are missing in the original colour. If this is so it means that in response to the percept of say magenta the eye's activity brings towards that percept the activity that is missing, in this case green, thereby completing the spectrum. The eye becomes active in order to reunite with the percept that part of the full light spectrum which is missing.

Here we see the eye acting in the same way as the human being does in the act of knowledge as developed by Goethe which reunites percept and concept. As the eye 'lays on top' (Diana Pauli) of the original percept the complementary colour, so it is possible in the act of cognition to experience that within our souls there arises a corresponding inner activity through which we can reunite what has been torn asunder by our organization. This is fundamental to the worldview which Goethe and Steiner developed: to experience this as fully as possible is the path of knowledge.

The experience of the activity of the eye in producing the complementary colour is a sense-perceptible phenomenon, readily accessible to anyone, which demonstrates an objective etheric dynamic. As such it could be an accessible 'portal' to the functioning of the etheric.

This points towards the activity of the soul in the act of knowledge, as practiced by Goethe and described by Steiner, being an action of the etheric. Both in nature and in the human being this principel holds good and could, I think, be useful in becoming clearer about the action and nature of the etheric. It seems to me to be an 'open secret' that has been under our nose, or rather on either side of it!

What excites me about this is that through connecting the experience I have of the way that a complementary colour arises in me in response to focusing on a sense-perceptible colour I find that my experience correlates with that which arises within my soul in response to outer phenomena and which I have learnt, after 27 years of working, to recognise as a path to higher truths. I am not suggesting that seeing complementary colours is the same as the act of cognition; only that here we may be experiencing, sense-perceptively, the purest expression of the etheric dynamic.

In speaking to Nick Weidemann he pointed out that the way a Newtonian physicist thinks about a colour, say magenta, is that it absorbs all of the light spectrum except the one which we perceive. He went on to point out that the idea that the eye through its activity actually supplies what is lacking in the percept still applies, as long, that is, as the complementary colour supplies the rest of the spectrum. In the 1918 addition to his chapter 'Are there limits to knowledge?' Steiner writes that 'thinking leads us into that part of the reality which the percept conceals within itself' (p.106 *Philosophy of Freedom,* where, interestingly, Steiner is talking about light to illustrate his ideas).

There is a correspondence for me, as an English teacher, to the activity that I have observed when we see a one-sided work of art, theatre, poem, etc. In this situation we are stimulated to become inwardly active to bring the 'complementary' part of the spectrum to it which is missing from the picture of humanity being presented and thereby 'healing' the one-sidedness.

No wonder art therapy works so well.

This would corroborate our understanding that the etheric tends towards wholeness and healing.

This is a very imperfect attempt on my part to try to formulate the idea which came to me in response to Diana Pauli's beautifully clear characterization and demonstration of the phenomenon of colour. When I mentioned it to Diana after the lecture she said that she had not thought of it that way before. I have written this in the hope of stimulating both discussion of the phenomena and constructive criticism of the way in which I have tried to formulate the idea and hoping that people will point out any glaring errors I have made!

Liz Attwell: August 2012

Explanation: The eye overlaying a colour with the complementary colour—to complete the spectrum.

18th Oct

The place from which I am viewing the mental pictures—of reflected sunlight—are behind the sun.

Inspirational thinking is alchemy of the soul. Cold thought passed through the heart into the cauldron of the desires and instincts connecting with purified warmth rises up to light up the stars of the cosmic etheric body to create a 'firmament fretted with golden fire' (*Hamlet*). (!!)

Essay

Ken Robinson identifies a problem—split between science and art.

Goethe's scientific work straddled those. Investigate his approach.—Link to lesson on the end of 'Midsummer Night's Dream.'

27th Oct

Goethe's scientific approach is the basic building block of genuine, experience-based enquiry.

APPLY AT ALL TIMES!

31st Oct

Goethe's method relies on building up observation and facts until you can move through the frozen moments in time, backwards and forward, to experience the whole plant (play) in movement.

The forces which are not visible but are causing an equal and opposite reaction in the physical—need to be experienced. (?)

30th Nov

In World Economy XIII Steiner shows positive
Nature x Labour used = Value
Spirit—Labour saved = Value
This is the eye of the plant!!! Effective spirit creates a new eye for new growth.

3 things are opening up to me:

1. Anthroposophy is beginning to move.
2. I am beginning to be able to connect this to my experience in teaching.
3. I *may* (or not) be able to begin to build a bridge to the mainstream.

These are in order of importance. I must nurture my anthroposophy and the others will follow (?).

11th Nov

Literature is a magic carpet which whisks you to new worlds—needs a Phoenix, the Spirit to work.

The 'Typus' in Goethean organic science corresponds to genre in Literature. The Archetype.

In child development.

Root–cotyledon -	0–7
Stem/leaves	7–14
Flower	14–21
Fruit	21–42 (?)
Dying/Blessing	42 –

15ᵗʰ Nov

In *Goethean Science* (Steiner's introductions to Goethe's Scientific work) Steiner quotes/describes how Goethe read bones 'as a text'—just as images and ideas arise as a result of reading a text.

With texts I read the structure just like the bones to find the spiritual realities within.

(p. 26) 'I consider the boney system to be the basic sketch of the human being.'

'Fleshy parts are colour on this drawing.'

(p. 27) Goethe writes to Lavater and Merk on 14 November 1781 that he is treating 'bones as a text to which everything living and everything human can be appended.'

'As we consider a text, pictures and ideas take shape in our spirit that seem to be called forth, to be created by the text.' Steiner (p. 27)

(p. 37) 'If he had written a book Goethe's work would give us an arche-typical model of how to find the laws of objective contemplation of the world.'

Discovery of skull bones as modified vertebrae.

(p. 45) 'Every living thing in its power to form and give shape to itself from within outward.'

(p. 53) 'Spinoza talked of 3 kinds of knowledge:

—Recall

—Forming general concept

—A knowledge of the being of things.' Scientia intuitive *Knowledge in beholding*

Spinoza—recognises certain aptitudes of God. Spinoza's God in the idea—content of the world. Steiner says 2 ways of looking at it:

1. God remains untouched
2. God is poured out—had laid itself, its own being and life, into the creation in such a way that it now exists only within the creation.

(p. 54) 'Our activity of knowing must then mean a becoming aware of that infinite within the things.'

'To see God in nature, nature is God.'
Essay: Power to Judge in Beholding. Goethe
'The adventure of reason' Goethe.
'We would make ourselves worthy, through beholding an ever-creating nature of participating spiritually in its productions.'

22nd Nov

Etheric Knowing is like an *inner sunrise*.

5th Dec

Reading Theosophy I realise that all these 'worlds' that Steiner describes after death—interpenetrate us *now*. When we are experiencing spiritual realities embedded in texts we are operating in metaphor and symbolism on several levels—resonating back and forth, between multiple levels of soul and spirit archetypes—hence the powerful, transformative experience—lifted out of the body into soul and spirit worlds.

23rd Dec

In the Paradise Play. In Genesis—Eden has the tree of life and the tree of Knowledge of good and evil. Lucifer tempts Eve and when Adam eats he feels naked—self conscious. This is the astral body entering too early—the stream of the astral—Lucifer opened our eyes too early.

We are expelled from Eden—away from the tree of life. God says we will be able to return 'late and slow' (the Oberaufer Play).

To return we must perceive below the surface of things—to penetrate to an awareness of the etheric in the moment. This is a pillar—within us—poured into the physical body all the time.

We perceive the material world but we begin to have direct percepts from the spiritual world—this is where intuition always comes from—and is also percept- forming whole.

This *is* the Tree of Life. In Roslin Chapel the Apprentice pillar is said to contain the Holy Grail. It is carved in the form of the tree of life. (Ta-da!)

I have come into the presence of the Grail.

27th Dec

The Lord's Prayer [pencil original]

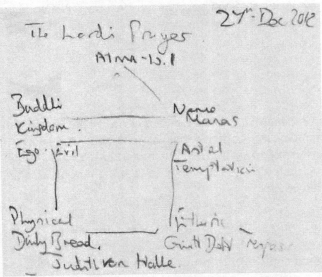

Transforming the Tree of Knowledge within you into the flourishing Tree of Life. When Spirit Self/Manas begins to develop then there begins to be the perception of the intrinsic names of things (like Google-glasses(!)). This is the beginning of transforming knowledge into the Tree of Life.

'All occult training takes place in the etheric body.'—R.S, 1907

'The etheric body is also the bearer of memory as a capacity, not as the memorizing of things. For instance if your memory needs to be made more acute this involves changing the etheric body. If it fades, it is a change in your etheric body, a change in your ability to memorize.' (p. 34)

(p. 47) 'The least like a natural force is thinking. Counting and calculating is furthest removed from what goes on in nature... If you were to go back far enough you would find beings (the spiritual ancestors of humanity) for whom, compared to us, it would have been complete nonsense to say that they formed concepts of external objects. For they would have "seen" the concept as an activity, even as a being.'

2nd Jan 2013

All this activity in me is a result of 2 things.

1. Before children I could induce a 'lifting' out of my body—(about 2 inches) in relaxation or meditation. After menopause (Sept 2011) this began to happen involuntarily when I was relaxing

(sometimes associated with a clenching of the womb and hot flush—mostly not). Now it is happening more and more frequently—relaxing, meditating and in conversation.

2. I am 52. I have studied Anthroposophy for 26 years. For 26 years materialism built up scales over my eyes. It has taken 26 years to remove them.

Lectures in Hanover

7th Jan

Yesterday I *realised* that if memory is a capacity of reflecting the Akashic record—then God is a dynamic that we perceive.

I work on the 6th of Jan.—the culmination of the Holy Nights that Brien Masters suggested I take my work into with the thought 'Carpe Diem'—A motto for the year?

27th Jan

I want to record an event on my birthday 14th June 2012. I woke—and experience a rush of joy connected to my birth 52 years before—I felt that this was my mother's joy. Even while I was feeling it—I began to calculate how many years it was since she died in 1999-13—I subtracted 3x13 = 39 from 1999 -> 1960—the year of my birth! Mother has arrived in Karma Loca—(reverse time x3 the hour of sleep) at my birth!!!

I could not stop myself calculating even though I knew I should wait and enjoy the joy as it flowed—I do have the feeling it subsided quicker than it could have. A beautiful feeling.

30th Jan

Simultaneously in class 12 J. (a pupil) and K. (another pupil) had 2 a-ha moments. J. that the Pardoner is God in this role—K. that the Pardoner is playing the Devil. Both right!

1st Feb

The Science of Knowing (p. 58)

Intellect and Reason. There are two ways of thinking intellect—(analysis) that separates and Reason which joins.

Intellect—Verstand

Reason—Vernunft

1ˢᵗ stage and 3ʳᵈ stage Goetheanism. That is why walking—activity is so important to joined up thinking.

(p. 67) 'Our spirit is not to be seen as a receptacle for the world of ideas—containing the thoughts within itself, but better as an organ that perceives these thoughts. This is an organ of apprehension in exactly the same way as the eyes and ears are. A thought relates itself to our spirit in no other way than light does to the eye and sound to the ear.' etc .

Here he states it the most clearly I have ever found it.

6ᵗʰ Feb

From an essay on the Etheric Heart by Ruth Haertl*
    Study of the Etheric Heart. Steiner draws the new etheric heart

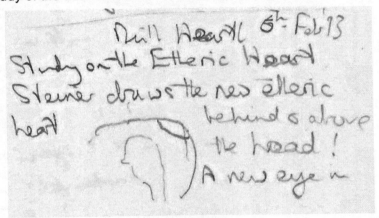

Behind and above the head! A new eye in the spirit! This is what I describe when I describe when I think about thinking—and have experienced for 26 years.

What matters is not to be original, but to be inwardly active.

9ᵗʰ June

The senses of movement, balance and life are released at the change of teeth (These are mathematising senses before that work on the body). At puberty—these are released from feeling and willing. I think they metamorphose into—sense of speech, thought and ego. After formation of the etheric heart.

---

*A Study of The Formation of a New Etheric Heart Organ in the Light of the Present Michaelic Mystery Culture as Rudolf Steiner Required it for our Age (2000) Trans. Monica Gold.

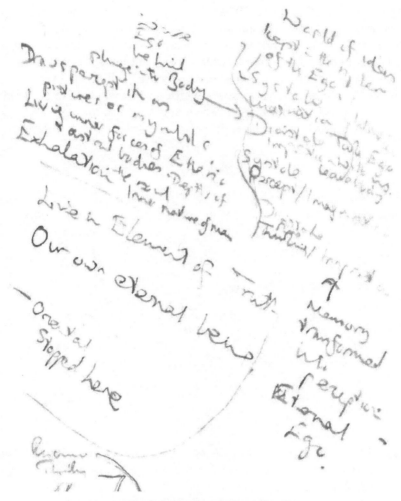

[facsmile of pencil original]

They are freed to the three upper senses. Hence independent judgment can arise.

How?

Through inner activity. Here the senses are also the thinking in itself???

Is this how the subject/object dichotomy is overcome?

Speech—sense of Balance (?)

Thought—Movement

Ego—The other, Life

Break through to a realm where we are reunited.

Boundaries of Natural Science. Lecture VIII and others

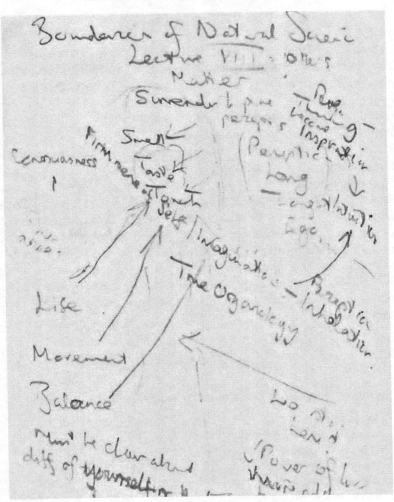

[facsmile of pencil original]

29th July 2013

My daughter says she is giving up on our relationship. I wrote:

Dear ....,

I am very sorry that you feel that I am not a good mother. It makes me sad and afraid that we will not be able to heal this. I will love you whatever. It is a privilege to be your mother.

All my love, Mum x

29th August

To understand ourselves we must look out. The cosmos is god/ourselves poured out. Every aspect can be read as part of the cosmic script, to understand ourselves. The way light works tells us who we are, and how Spirit works

(What are black holes?).

Written 25th August in Edinburgh on notes

It was Roman Catholicism that separated man from the spirit. Now Natural Science denies the validity of intuition—continuing the work of the Catholic Church.

Reading is the recreation of thoughts and feelings in the soul- causing 'flow' (discovered by the Hungarian psychologist Csíkszentmihályi). You can read the world recreating in thoughts and feelings (soul) the truths that it is expressing—this is the initiates script that Steiner describes in 'Occult Science' and everywhere else.

Re-call—memory is 'called' from the cloud through inner activity. It is no accident that the iCloud is called that, a lower technological picture of this activity.

Tues. 24th September

The morning verse contains all we need of Goethean Science.

I look into the world,
Wherein there shines the Sun
Wherein there gleam the stars
Wherein there lie the stones
Where living grow the plants
Where feeling live the beasts
And where in Man ensouled a dwelling to Spirit gives.

I look into the soul
Which dwelleth me within
God's Spirit lives and weaves
In light of Sun and Soul
In space of worlds without
In depths of Soul within
To Thee, O Spirit of God
I seeking turn
That Strength and Blessing May
For learning and for work
Within me live and grow.

Is the outer threshold a glass in which we see darkly? Do we extrapolate past that rather than stay with the phenomena and penetrate the other way into the soul?

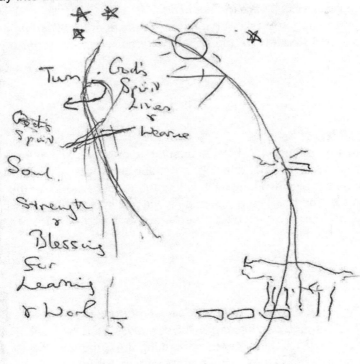

24th September

In *The Human Soul in Relation to World Evolution* Steiner says we realise 'with a jolt that we are behind the Sun.' This makes more sense if the sun is hollow—a reflector of light—a negative sun-space.

6th November

The Janus God with his two heads expresses the experience of standing at the threshold. Perceiving both ways.

8th Nov

Today spoke in Study mandate about the way that AS students learn— through coursework—to develop a capacity for 'spirit-vision.' Used the term and realised that, presumptuous though it sounds,—it does describe what they are doing. There is a definite process they have to learn of discovering what they have to do to study a text and subject until they begin to 'see' a pattern begin to coalesce in their minds.

F. and H. began to talk with authority today about *A Midsummer Night's Dream*—and I could see the capacity formed in them. What a privilege to be there.

10th Nov

The Science of Knowing

(p.43) An opinion… 'There is absolutely only *one single* thought-content, and our individual thinking is nothing more than our self, our individual personality, working its way into the *thought-centre* of the world.'

If this is true (it is) then a text, as a window into the thoughts and feelings of an individual—is also a portal to the thought centre of the world (which is Christ).

11th Nov

Thinking is the core of the World (*Science of Knowing* p.70)

(p.73) 'Through our thinking we lift ourselves from the view of reality as a product to a view of reality as something that produces.'

We are become Gods—co-creators with the divine.

(p.74) 'The form of reality that the human being produces in science is the ultimate, true form of reality.'

17th Nov

Surely Vygotsky's *Zones of Proximal Development* suggests a process of a pre-existing entity outside the body of the child which is in a process of incarnation (?).

Horizons of development rather than goals (A central tenet of my tutor at King's College London based on Vygotsky's work)

7th December

When a lecturer speaks from the Akashic record, people report they look over their heads 'as if at a panorama unfolding just above and behind the audience. Actually they are looking inside—just as far.

24th February 2014

Is there an analogy between meeting of matter and anti-matter and percept and concept which release energy as light?—Then reform as new? Matter?

25th Feb

In *The Child's Changing Consciousness* R.S. says that the change of teeth is like a glass of water with sediment settling—so that the child can think. Before that the child is all sense organ.

When we are upset—say in an accident, thinking becomes difficult because the sediment is disturbed.

That was how I felt after the biographical weekend at the Social Development Centre; as if the sediment was stirred up and would settle into a new pattern. New possibilities for thinking.

16th March

Sediment idea—talking about Eurythmy in the U.S. and Formative Assessment—I realised that movement arts are, of course, working with all

12 senses and therefore working with the sediment mixed into the water—as in Kindergarten—using all 12 senses. The ideal of teaching in U.S. is to engage all 12. In my essay—or maybe dissertation—This needs reflecting.

15th June

Ideas for INSETT demonstration
  Light demonstration
  Apercu/Apperception
  Insight—Perceptive
  Advert or revelation

  Carol Dweck—Austin's Butterfly (youtube)
  Dorothy Heathcote—3 Looms Waiting (youtube)
  Ken Robinson—RSA animated talks
  CAN WE CREATE A 'SWOOSH'?
  Google Glasses. The Cloud.

16th June

Rumpelstiltskin is a story for our time.
  King: Lower Self—greedy for gold.
  Miller's Daughter—soul.
  Makes a pact with the devil to meet greed of king. The higher self as baby is threatened.
  Sends out Messenger—Intuition
  Finds his name.
  If we can name what is besieging us, it will tear itself in two.
  Attack is in technology and the economy. Ahriman.
  The title for the Workdays could be (School) 'Creating a Space for Self-Actualisation' (or the Conditions).

13th July

This Term I observed 2 class 8's:
8A is a healthy learning organism.
8B is not.
WHY?
My perception is that: 8A have the space to discover themselves in freedom. 8B do not. What I observe there is that due to the personality of the

teacher 'pressing' into the centre of their being the students are 'oppressed'— This means that they cannot incarnate in a healthy way and the energy 'splurges' out sideways into astral negativity that attacks from the periphery.

These students cover their faces with their hoods, slouch, and are passive-aggressive. They criticise each other and themselves and have low self-efficiency.

To turn this around would be an incredible achievement.

13th July

Reading about 12.12—the shift that happened. I looked back at what I was doing. The 23rd Dec 2012. The day Nostradamus was supposed to predict the end of the world is the day I wrote: I have come into presence of the Grail. Coincidence??

24th July

Looked it up it was 21.12.12. I was two days late!

27th July

From *The Festivals and their Meaning*
II: Whitsun.
The Festival of the Free Individuality
'You shall know the truth and the truth shall set you free,' Christ says of the Holy Spirit. Came in a dove at Baptism. In tongues of flame at Whitsun.
'The universal human spirit, which we recognise as the Whitsun power of the Holy Spirit entering into us, and which we must bring to birth within ourselves and allow to come to manifestation.'
The Aha! is the Holy Spirit entering us in self-actualisation—progressively making us free.
The ultimate intuition would be *Christ*.

29th July

Matthew 18:
The disciples came to Jesus, saying 'Who is the greatest in the Kingdom of Heaven?' And calling to him a child, he put him in the midst of

them and said, 'Truly, I say to you, unless you turn and become like children, you will never enter the Kingdom of Heaven.' …

Passage on not being the one to cause one of them to sin.—'Better to be drowned '

'See that you do not despise one of these little ones; for I tell you that in heaven their angels always behold the face of my Father, who is in heaven.'

2nd August

Lecture 7 of *Universal Spirituality and Human Physicality*—R.S.

'What, then, are we really doing in soul-spiritual terms when we develop love in ourselves, out of our will? We are forming *a spirit-soul after-image* within us, inside our skin, of what composed our whole being before we were conceived.' (p. 84)

21st August

In *In Search of Thinking* Richard Bunzl p. 87 says that what we see in the things is the inherent concept.

When we are aware that we do not understand something there is a tension, a sense of imbalance, and resolution brings symmetry.

'as a universal concept is individualised from out of the total in a universalised form, so the inherent concept towards which our consciousness is intended is universalised from out of the perceptible world fabric.'

'What is conceptually universal becomes specific; what is conceptually unique is given a universal form. Only in this meeting of the conceptual in thinking with the conceptual which permeates the world do we truly attain cognitive balance.'

'The nature of I-ness is to strive for cognitive resolution and balance, the result of which is consciousness itself.'

I woke up this morning realizing with renewed vigour the way that questions are posed by our body, by being in the world, and this knowing comes as an answer. Reading with our feeling is a sort of meditation in the middle.—They resonate.

25th August

Title for a new essay:

'Creating the Conditions for Intuitive Practice in Teaching.'

21st Aug on *The Educators* John Hattie was interviewed and said 'The thing that makes the most difference in teaching is the Teacher—their enthusiasm and empathy to "switch kids on" to learning.'

'We are talking about empowering Head Teachers, I find it incredible that there is no debate about how to empower the teacher in the classroom.'

'How do we make all teachers like the top 20-30%.'

13th Sept

In the workdays I deconstructed my 'Aha' essay. 8 concepts which I then created expert groups for. Could one deconstruct Steiner's essays in a similar way for teacher training? 'Deconstructing Steiner'! An essay?

Just as deconstructed theatre makes the viewer inwardly active and works with the afterimage. So deconstructing my essay created a space for the teachers to be inwardly active.

Derrida and 'difference' is working with this dynamic—I think.

1st Oct

I realised how much this inner activity would remove obstacles in the path of the child's growing-up which would make for long-term health benefits—very real.

3rd Oct

The Aha! is the new clairvoyance—absolutely clear seeing with total ego clarity.

26th Oct

A lecture entitled 'How to facilitate Steiner's Seeing Consciousness (*Schauendes Bewusstsein*) (*The Riddle of Man*) in Teenagers *and* get great Exam Results in English Lit. A-level!'

Vom Menchenrätsel 1916

Goethe's 'power to judge in beholding' p .135

Anshauende Urteilskraft

28th Nov

'Power to judge in beholding' allows ideas to be perceived 'as objects in space.'—hence—the inner dimensions of the inner space are opening up to us.

Lesson 8 in the first class—when you pass the threshold (the beasts) you enter into 3 dimensions—

Like the Renaissance—when perspective opened up. Now we are developing film and games. 3D

Keynote speech at Steiner House 27th June 2015

'*The Riddle of Man* (and developing the capacity for) developing the power to Judge in Beholding.' For Teenagers.

29th Nov

Revelations 22:

'The river of the water of life bright as crystal, flowing from the throne of God and of the Lamb.'

'On either side of the river—the tree of life with its 12 kinds of fruit, yielding its fruit each month and the leaves of the tree were for the healing of nations.'

14 'Blessed are those who wash their robes, that they may have the right to the tree of life and that they may enter the city by the gates.'

17 'Let him who is thirsty come, let him who desires take the water of life without price.'

18 'If anyone takes away from the words of this prophecy, God will take away his share in the tree of life and the holy city.'

24th Dec

Ivan Rioux In *New View Magazine*

In the past people perceived '*intelligent activity*' as beings e.g. Persephone and Demeter. This is called Myth. Today we must reverse this and perceive beings where now we see intelligent activity.

10th Jan 2015

The Tree of Knowledge is the realm of Ahriman. The tree of Life—Lucifer. The Guardian of the Threshold keeps us from the tree of life. The Greater Guardian allows us access and keeps the active balance—The Christ. 'Not I, but Christ in Me.'

I have just read about the lesser and greater Guardian in 'Knowledge of Higher Worlds' and have read:

'With the powers you have already achieved you may sojourn in the lower regions of the supersensible world; but before the portal of the higher I stand (as the Cherubin with the fiery sword before Paradise) and I forbid your entrance as long as you retain powers that have not been put to use in the sense-world.' (p. 210)—*Knowledge of the Higher Worlds*

11th Jan

The Representative of Man is an A-ha moment in statue form!!!

And

In the lecture 'Where is the Tree of Life?'—Dornach, July 24, 1915, Steiner lays down a clue. He says

there is the 'greatest riddles' [*sic*] is 'the Christ riddle' and 'this Christ riddle *is* (his emphasis) a riddle.' He

uses riddle 15 times in the 1st 3 paragraphs. Then starts talking about the 2 trees.

2nd Feb

Steiner named his magazine 'Lucifer' because he was pointing to the Tree of Life that is Lucifer's domain.(?)

The Christ activity.

(p. 53) The Tree of Life and the Tree of Knowledge.

Christ activity is holding apart the sense perceptions and the 'shining from behind.' The concepts 'Lucifer mixes together ideas concepts and sense perception.'

10th Feb

How to support self-actualisation in CPD?

In teaching it is by creating a 'negative space' into which the children can incarnate. It seems to me that CPD is just the same. Create a protected 'negative space' for the other—a womb—into which they can conceive themselves.

14th Feb

Whilst searching (desperately) for a suitable Valentines card for Nic this morning I came across a card of a painting of Luca Signorelli—*The Lamentation for Christ*. I realised that I was looking at a depiction of the holy grail and that the secret of the descent of Christ's blood from the head to the heart—resurrects as the tree of life in Saint John in the painting.

It feels incredible that a process that I described 2.5 years ago as one my students were waking up to, was depicted 500 years ago (1505) in a painting clearly representing the Holy Grail—with the Crucifixion, Descent from the Cross, and Resurrection forming a chalice—which contains the water of life—the cross with the blood flowing down—the tree of life growing up and the New Jerusalem!!!!

16ᵗʰ Feb

I woke up realising that my child should have had Anthro. speech therapy. Could still have, if I found a way. I realised how different he could have been if I lived my life through intuition.

We are all Faustus, making little pacts with the devil instead of really living. Life is asking of me so much more than I am giving.

20ᵗʰ Feb

I could write an article about the tree of life—the a-ha moment—and Signorelli's painting.

24ᵗʰ Feb

A fabulous four days. The weekend on Child Study with Christof Weichert—Profound Goethean study of children. Then a day on Non-Violent Communication.

The four steps Observation: Feeling, Needs/Values, Action have a relationship to Goethean Science.

The searching for universal human values beneath the needs is a real bringing into realization of the social Etheric. 'The healthy social life… etc.'

It freed the individual from the double—projected out onto the world. Jackal response was the double. The Giraffe response was out of a higher self.

4ᵗʰ March

Looking at Signorelli's 'The Lament for the Dead Christ' I realise that the water of life is the lower etheric. It becomes the tree of life when vivified by inner activity it climbs upwards—through the para-sympathetic nerve system (arts, physical expression) and reaches out to light up the whole aura. It is this process of inspiration, then the Christ appears in the human being. At peak moments we are doing this in English.

1st August

Reading Occult Science this summer holiday—I realise that I am meeting the Higher Guardian of the Threshold through my students. — When insight, drenched in new morality appears—There he is. Also that Steiner warns that the 'pupil's' courage may fail him. He needs to say 'I am not going to stand still.' This is where I am—faltering—and using tactics not to go on. I need to find the strength to take myself in hand. The Greater Guardian says 'press forward with untiring energy' (p. 293).

Otherwise this new world you have discovered will change into illusion. The Greater Guardian is the "Ideal, the Example" that he will do his utmost to follow.' The figure of the Christ.

—Finishes with 'It is of vital importance that at every stage harmony should reign between man's life in the world at large and the Way of Initiation.' (p. 297)

The trials (inner) that my pupils go through are more real than anything else, I realise—this is because we are operating in Ahriman's realm—and they have to face the scalding rain of possible failure and inner shame—to transmute it into a realization of real learning.

15th Oct

Our 27th wedding anniversary—spent at school! College has given support for the Christchurch masters to be run at the school.

14th Nov

Went to Denmark. Michael Brinch brought a picture of the Aha! !!
Child meets the world says Ah da?
When finds concept Aha!
As we 'grow up' we make assumptions and do not reach all the way forward or back.—harden—at its worst, fundamentalism.

Michael Brick brought a
picture of the Aha! !!

— Child's Boundary

Meets
the
sense
world

— Meets
the Inner
~~Spirit~~ World

Crossing point
like human being

Child meet Flk world says Ah da?
When finds concept Aha!
As we "grow up" we make

My picture: When I have an Aha! I feel like this

My picture :—
When I have an Aha!, I feel
like this

Sense World   Spiritual World.

no — I think in peak moments
the lemniscate inverts

Drop of light

and opens out to infinity
on both sides — from primal
beginnings to primal distances
and a drop of light from the
spirit of our age ~~experienced~~
contained.

So—I think in peak moments the lemniscates inverts

And opens out to infinity on both sides—from primal beginnings to primal distances and a drop of light from the spirit of our age /conceived.

Afterwards we have grown and risen—the circle in which the/our lemniscates operates is bigger—and we have stepped up. I should try to talk to Michael about this.

'The fire and the rose are one.' *Four Quartets*

Answers to Journaling q's from Learning from the Emerging Future (p. 172)

1. My teaching of teenagers is dying (?)
     My teaching of adults is being born.
2. Guardian Angels are Nic, Josie, Dorothy Heathcote, Steiner, Mum.
3. Investigating. Creativity
4. The lack of meaningful contact with my children. The lack of meaningful contact with my colleagues.
5. To be with my husband—To teach
6. Take the step to universalise my teaching
7. Renew ourselves
8. How do I make meaningful contact?
9. Stop talking so much, listen more.
10. More light
11. Lighten up!
12. Intensify my creativity—and communicate it to others.
      Warmer home emotionally—more cooking
      More joyful in my work—do what I love.
      More integrated social life—sing.
      Enough energy for all these
13. Be free—stop being superior.
14. A study group.
15. Catherine, Davina, Andrew.
16. Email Otto!!!

6ᵗʰ Dec

St Nicholas Day
Journaling answers from Theory U—p. 253 'Leading from...'

1. Openness
2. More open, vibrant situation.
3. Ownership
4. How close opening could be.
5. That, maybe, I could make this step—that I need to.

6. The vision of the commons.
7. Sharing
8. Creative meeting
9. Alistair, Davina, William, Catherine
10. Reading, Bothmer, Yoga, Walks, thinking—need to meditate—singing
11. By the above—need to sing, more and speech
12. Email Otto. Talk to Peter. Talk to Nic

19th Dec

While singing at the Forest Row Choral Soc. Concert for Christmas I realised that the book that I am reading Reinventing Organizations feels like such a party in my heart because it is showing how organisations can run in a way that honours the Tree of Life within each one of us.—and can give it the opportunity for expression.

5th Jan 2016

Could the double helix of DNA be a pictorial microcosm of the Tree of Life? Could that be reflected in the staff of Life? Esoteric Knowledge of the upwardly spiralling motion of the T. of L?

5⁵ Jan 2016.

Could the double helix of DNA be a pictorial microcosm of the Tree of Life? Could that be reflected in the Staff of Life ⚕ ? Esoteric ⚕ Knowledge of the upwardly spiralling motion of the T. of L? Incidentally—the question mark shows the oscillation (maybe?) —or at least the receptivity in its cupped form.

Incidentally the question mark shows the oscillation (maybe?)—or at least the receptivity in its cupped form.

2nd April

There are two thresholds.
Between Tree of Knowledge and the Tree of Life.

	Knowledge	Tree of Knowledge
Lesser Guardian -------------------------		
	Embodied Knowing	Tree of Life
Greater Guardian------------------------------		
	Transcendence	Spiritual World

Then between the Tree of Life and the further spiritual world?

6th May

By taming the dragon the fruits can flourish.—12 different for each month
The Apprentice Pillar at Roslyn

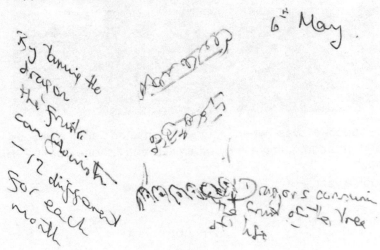

Dragons consuming the fruit of the Tree of Life.
The first threshold was crossed when Cambridge teachers sat in a circle—and David started to say the truth from the interview he had done—Lesser Guardian.

The second was when they reconnected and everyone had stepped into community—they all smiled and no one spoke.—Higher Guardian.

It took a year.

20th Aug

The Rod of Hermes—Trismegistus—The Caduceus

Have I discovered the rod of Hermes? I googled that and got this. Do the wings denote the higher self.

Nic's reaction: 'It is about becoming Gods.'

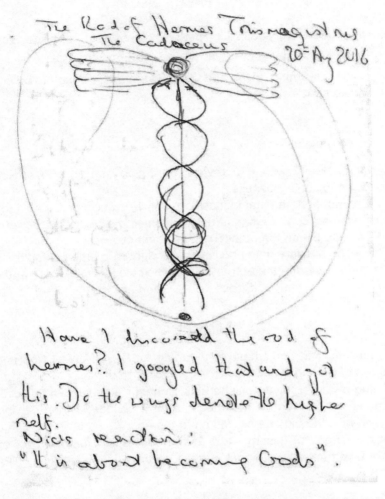

The metamorphosis of the lower into the higher self? Could the snakes be the Tree of Life—on either side of the Water of Life (the spinal fluid) in a picture of the transformed human being? (*Book of Revelation*).

24th July

Reading *Goethe's World View* again—it dawns on me that our perception is always 'sensible-supersensible' as Steiner describes it. This means that we are viewing the sense-perceptible from eternity—from beyond space and time—it's just that we are unconscious of it. (!!!)

12th August

After the Theory U crystallisation process I have 2 strong images/concepts

1. CARE
2. We are learning driven and we need to break through to an interpersonal space.

27th August

I woke up today with a renewed realization that light is analogically connected to consciousness.

—So I appreciated that just as light only becomes visible as it touches an object—so consciousness only becomes visible in the act of attention—as it lands on the object of consciousness.

To become aware of the activity of the light is to step behind the sun—to become aware of the eternity from which we view the 'here and now'

'Space   and   Time

21st September

It is four fifty AM and I have lit a candle for David Attwell who is in the process of leaving this world.

Lying awake, I have realised that Michael Hall is also in this process. Perhaps we can form a new heart, a 'new college,' which can start to beat—whilst the old one carries on to the end.

A new organ of destiny—just as the adolescent forms a new etheric heart. One that will reconnect with the parent body too. A new PTFA.

4th Oct

Woke up with the question 'What does *real* education look like?'
   Like an internal sunrise. Like the real bread on a real table.
   Connect moments of real education and build a picture.
   To *be* or not to *be*, that is the question.

13th June 2017

Things to Do!!!

1. Organise Sept. Workdays
2. Organise Nov 4th conference
3. ?

23rd June 2017

A long break in inspirations! Was the dissertation so destructive?

I have become Education Section Coordinator—and have to work out what that means.

Yesterday had an inspiration—maybe!

3-fold Social Order talked about in College. Andrew Scott talked about

Economy	–	Process	–	Working Hands
Rights	–	Structure	–	Timetable
Culture	–	Relationships	–	What we say and wear

Pretty mundane—maybe?

I thought about Holacracy.

Drew a connection—3 leafed clover? Looked Complex

Also means potential for an a-ha moment where both external sides meet!!! School forms a heart! Who should be on college becomes central.

10th July

One week ago today I saw my son off at 5am and went back to bed. I felt an 'abnormality' in my breast. Now I am concerned it is cancerous. Trying to get it investigated. Meanwhile...

Contemplating the limb in Foundations of Human Experience—and the idea that it also has a chest and head!?? Radical inversion—I am remembering the clay modelling I did with Martin Hardiman where a skull bone metamorphoses into a leg/arm bone.

Feb 12th 2018

The sun has risen North of Peter and Pauline's Christmas Tree, and I am resurrecting from surgery and emerging from chemo into the light.

June 14th

My 58th Birthday! What a year it has been—very intense and hard too. I am grateful to have reached this place.

This morning woke up to a clear conviction that as Ed. Section Coordinator... I must stay out of the exoteric part of the Movement. Do not mix it up with the fellowship!!!

I am reaching the conviction that I need a complete break with school—and time—to play. So—I feel very lucky to have that as a goal!

It occurred to me that the exoteric gets mixed in the physical—which is, by its very nature finite—while the esoteric should connect at least to the etheric—which has infinite abundance. That is the most useful role that I can play in the movement—if I can strengthen the connection to the soul/spiritual. Everything else is a distraction! And everything must proceed from JOY!

23rd July

Have read Craig Holdrege's *Thinking Like a Plant*. Revelatory—and at the same time—familiar.

He shows how thinking develops like a plant—with 'exact sensorial imagination' putting out leaves and roots—then flower comes—Inspiration—the Ümstulpung—creates a chalice (calyx?) which allows the fertilisation to occur (the drop of light/intuition) which bear fruit—they have a generative nature—they bear the seeds of new life?

I realise that the apprentice pillar in Roslyn shows the Holy Grail—because it shows dragons—out of whose mouths the Tree of Life grows. It bears no fruit—the dragons consume the fruit.

This coincides with the diagram of reaction/response.

The energy of the lower self is transformed into activity which creates the chalice and allows fructification? The energy of the dragons becomes the possibility to fruit!!!

29th July

In conversation with Philip Kilner and others realised that 'Presencing' is a metamorphosis of the capacity of memory.

In 4th Class lesson R.S. says that 'what you normally call your memory… is only meant for earthly concerns and not for the concerns of the gods.'

That is why Gandalf in *Lord of the Rings* can hardly remember who he was after he goes to the next stage from Gandalf the Grey to Gandalf the White.

Steiner also says that overcoming sympathy and antipathy helps you grasp esoteric truth in our 'innermost soul, at the deepest level of our soul life where memory lives.' (p. 54)

16th August

A year ago today had my mastectomy.

Reading *The Psychological Foundations of Anthroposophy*—realised with this and conventional stuff on qualitative research and action research—I could relaunch the Ed. Section at Easter. Title: ' D.I.Y. Spiritual Action Research.'

Create a pack and an intro.

- Generate questions through activity
- Find approaches
- Meet 6 monthly

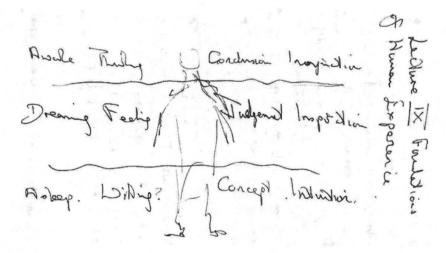

The upcoming generation—of teachers—et al—need Anthroposophy delivered in a different way. They need it to be experiential—delivered by people in whom it *moves*—it is *digested*—it has been assimilated—and they have become one with it.

If you can assimilate it, and then bring it to them transformed into food—experience—informed by your experience—and authentic—then they might be able to use the writings to verify *their* experience—From our heads to our hearts. Not so much the other way around.

—Their children will need it transformed in the heart to be able to take it into their will (?).

Lecture IX Foundations of Human Experience

31st August

In *The Psychological Basis of Spiritual Science* 1911 (April 8th) Steiner speaks about inspired knowing in terms of overcoming the subject/object divide (Aha!). It 'condenses itself, so to speak, through soul energy'—one becomes aware of an entity between the physical and the astral—the etheric body. What the self lives in as if in a being free of the physical, is an 'astral body."

'It is this ether body that provides the forces that enable the self to objectively perceive subjective, inspired Knowledge... this is how it works, because we experience the ether body as a confluence of the all-encompassing complex of macrocosmic principles.' (p. 35)—Esoteric Development.

1st September

THIS IS MASSIVE!

Because it means that (I realised this morning) the 'Representative of Man' shows this—the Christ sphere breaking through Ahriman and Lucifer's stronghold—to arrive at contemplation of the etheric; to 'objectively perceive subjective, inspired Knowledge' (p. 35—Esoteric Development).

At the Goetheanum we can spend time contemplating the Rep. of Humanity.

3rd September

I am getting answers to questions I have barely formulated!

Today (Esoteric De./Psycho Foundations Anthro p. 39). A description of the meeting with the Higher Guardian—Intuition—

—Ether body is differentiated, and lawful

—'Essential to the unification of its activity is a tendency to relate to something as a centre,' and the image of this unifying tendency is the physical body. This the physical body proves to be an expression of the universal 'I' (Christ).

Then goes on to talk about the way memory is changed.

8th Oct

Dad's 20th Death Day.

Woke up—and a few seconds later 'heard' the words 'I love you' very clearly and knew that they were 'spoken' by someone else. Only that evening, in retrospect, came to the conclusion, in light of the day, that they are from Dad.

15th Oct

Our 30th Wedding Anniversary.—We had Tim, Gin, Mark, Charlotte, Adam, Annabel, Graham, Kate and Andy for dinner. I was in great pain from my pelvis—realising this might be bone cancer.

19th Oct

MRI scan at short notice—think it might be bone cancer—digesting this thought together.

Sunday 21st Oct

Yesterday I drove to the top of 12 acre field (I could not walk it)—and did my meditation on the Lord's Prayer and Bothmer gym. At the end I cleared my mind and asked if the 'universe' had anything to say to me.

The answer was 'This will bring you to a meeting with the Christ' and 'It will strip everything down to the essential.' Pretty clear.

Wed 26th Dec

I got my diagnosis of bone cancer—and, more of a shock—liver cancer on 2nd Nov. It has been quite difficult since. Tried to go to Watergate bay—had to bale out—vomited up chemo—now calmer—on steroids and chemo + hyperthermia + cannabis for 60 days to see if we can buy time.

Meanwhile… reading 'From Jesus to Christ' (2011 GA131?) realised an 'Aha!': The Christ Event has meant Aha! possible.

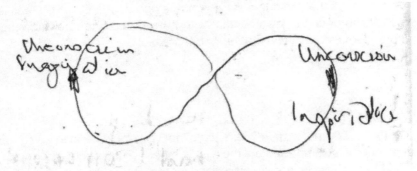

Lecture in Munich, May 1st, 1918. Archive 3515
p. 54 R. Steiner on *The Philosophy of Freedom*

'An idea, born of the immortal world that we experience before our birth, works in concert with the immortal element that manifests itself on an unconscious level in imagination and returns again into the spiritual world through the gate of death.'

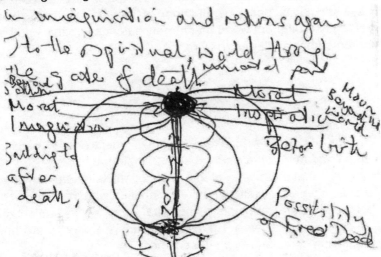

'Thus man is capable of actions in which his immortal part, otherwise revealed only after death, becomes an effective force during his earthly life and works in concert with free ideas issuing, through inspiration, from the immortal realm in the form of impulses that enter our human personalities before birth. This is then free deed.'

'Mortal man is en route to freedom.'

3rd March 2019

Off to go to Watergate Bay. Hope we have better luck this time.

Yesterday—an A-ha!

Goethe says that 'colour is the sufferings and deeds of light.' Realised light invisible until it makes contact with the world, so too our sufferings and deeds make our universal humanity visible!

4th March

Otto Palmer

On *Phil. Of Freedom*, p. 45, R.S. says that you would need to go beyond the planetary system 'to find the world where living thoughts apply'—beyond Saturn 'but where we also discover the cosmic source of creativity on earth.' Then the opposite 'so one can advance on the opposite side by entering deeply into the will to the extent of becoming utterly quiescent.'

p. 46 'When this happens, one comes out on the opposite side of the world.'

Feb 6th 1923 'endowed with its external character by the physical moon.' One learns to say 'You harbour in your will sphere a great variety of drives, instincts and passions. But none of them belongs to the world… They belong to a different world that merely extends into this one.'…'We begin to remember earlier earth lives.'

2nd July

My sister's birthday.

At Whitsun—9th June—I spoke about the 7th seal of the Apocalypse. Afterwards I had an Aha! talking to Laura Manning.

Steiner says that the picture of the 7th seal depicts the human being at the end of time when we will be 'entirely identified with the cosmos.'

A-ha Moments are moments of mystical unity, when subject/object divide is overcome…'They are each a step on the way to the human being identifying completely with the cosmos.'

I told my daughter, who was impressed, but added that it was 'obvious really'—which it is!

Still 2ⁿᵈ of July

I have often pondered the relationship between 'flow' and 'Aha'—both moments of subject/object divide being overcome—but very different too. Suddenly realised that Steiner says that there are 2 poles—when the life forces at the will pole—inner-growth, maintenance, reproduction, secretion, are the more active—it results in artistic creativity—'flow.'

When the 'outer 3 life processes predominate, warmth, breathing, nutrition, it tends more towards aesthetic appreciation,—Aha!

Pleased to have realised this.

Fri 12ᵗʰ July

4am in the morning. Nic and I went to *Rusalka* at Glyndebourne last night—sublime and engaging and beautiful.

Now, I am waking with the realization that there are signs of my liver swelling with the reduction of steroids—so coming to terms with the fact that this really might be the beginning of the end. I feel sad to be leaving so much behind—my beautiful family—the warmth of my friends—but grateful, also, that there might be a bearable way out of this life being presented to me.

What a journey!

Dawn Chorus just beginning.

Just had a solitaire/patience solve itself in one with greater simplicity than ever before!!!

Liz died on 2 September 2019.

Appendix One

COMPARE AND CONTRAST THE CONSTRUCTION OF 'OTHERNESS' IN *FRANKENSTEIN* AND *REGENERATION*

Introduction and conclusion from an A2 essay by Laura Manning
(a former student)

Introduction

The 'Other' refers to who, and what, is alien and divergent from the Self. The poet Rimbaud may be the earliest to express the idea: *'Je est un autre'*, literally, 'I is an other' thereby meaning, as Jacques Lacan said: 'The "I" is always in the field of the Other.' This can be elucidated: to be aware of one's own Self, one must be aware that we are 'Other' from everyone and everything else, we are surrounded by 'Other.' The philosopher, Hegel, states: 'Self-consciousness only achieves its satisfaction in another self-consciousness.' Mary Shelley and Pat Barker construct 'Otherness' throughout their novels to explore the nature of the human being; but also how 'Otherness' can be taken to an extreme, resulting in 'Othering', where those in power emphasize the 'perceived weaknesses' of others to portray them as not only 'other', but inferior.

Conclusion

Through *Frankenstein* I realized that the experience of Otherness is what offers the potential for evil, for only when one can see the beings in the world as 'Other' from oneself can one harm them. From *Regeneration* I came to the conclusion that making people 'Other' is an inbuilt way of coping with situations, and the pre-war civilization took this to an extreme. As human beings we are born at one with the world, but as we grow up we learn to distinguish between ourselves and the world. With this comes the potential for evil, but also the potential for love, for one could not love if one did not see others as 'Other', 'without a *you* and an *I*, there is no love' (Kierkegaard, *Works of Love*, p. 266). We see this in *Frankenstein* where the creature feels love for the cottagers despite feeling 'Other' from them, and in *Regeneration* in the loving paternal relationship Rivers has with his patients, which allows him to empathize with them. Therefore love could be what balances, or redeems, 'Otherness.' But the experience of 'Otherness' is an essential aspect of being human.

Appendix Two

COMPARE AND CONTRAST THE SIGNIFICANCE OF WINDOWS IN *FRANKENSTEIN* AND *WUTHERING HEIGHTS*

By India Ashe (a former student)

In Emily Brontë's *Wuthering Heights* and Mary Shelley's *Frankenstein* windows play a role in making physically manifest the separation of their protagonists from society. By utilizing setting as a means of conveying the emotions of its characters and of forewarning of key events, both Brontë and Shelley make use of window symbology. Whilst windows do not appear as frequently as other symbols such as moons, water, eyes, and fire, it is their consistent placement in important scenes that makes their presence so notable in the texts. In Shelley's *Frankenstein*, further examination of the context of window references can allow the reader to deepen their understanding of the relationship between Victor Frankenstein and the creature. In *Wuthering Heights*, Emily Brontë frequently makes use of windows to coincide with pertinent plot points as a vehicle for building or maintaining the tension present in the storyline. Likewise, in *Frankenstein*, Mary Shelley has them reflect the mental states of her main characters. This is particularly so for the creature, spending most of his life out of doors looking inward due to his separation from society.

Windows, in their most straightforward incarnation, are presented as physical barriers in both novels. Throughout *Wuthering Heights*, there is a constant power struggle over boundaries and barriers such as doors, gates, windows and locks, where certain characters exert their power over each other by confinement. The many characters frequent illnesses also mean the reader experiences this feeling of confinement in many senses. In his first descriptions of the house, Brontë's Lockwood observes its unwelcoming architecture: 'Happily, the architect had foresight to build it strong: the narrow windows are deeply set in the wall, the corners defended with large, jutting stones.' Constructed in 1500, this home is clearly designed to be impenetrable; even though Catherine's name is scratched on its surface, the window doesn't provide entry for her wailing ghost—mostly due to Lockwood's lack of sympathy. The bloodshed from Catherine's wrist 'rubbed [...] to and fro' across the windowpane demonstrates the serious violence accompanied with crossing thresholds. Lockwood wakes in the night to see the childlike ghost of Catherine Linton attempting to climb in through the window of her old room, in which Lockwood was staying the night.

Out of fear, Lockwood grabs her arm and slides her wrist over the broken windowpane, 'letting the blood flow down the window's recess.' Later in the novel, the young Cathy escapes Heathcliff from the same window: 'She dare not try the doors, lest the dogs should raise an alarm; she visited the empty chambers, and examined their windows; and luckily, lighting on her mother's, she got easily out of its lattice, and onto the ground by means of the fir tree, close by.'

One of the reasons windows are such a useful literary device in *Frankenstein* is because they set up a physical barrier between Victor and his creation. The first appearance of a window takes place when the creature comes to Frankenstein's apartment, the first time Victor has seen the creature since its awakening. Victor's fear is very evident: 'I started from my sleep with horror; a cold dew covered my forehead...by the dim and yellow light of the moon, as it forced its way through the window shutters, I beheld the wretch—the miserable monster whom I had created.' In both novels, the protagonists feel threatened from unwanted, unearthly visitors that they deem as unholy and dangerous. The fact that both the creature and Catherine Earnshaw's ghost attempt to gain admittance through the window shows their alienation from the world and in both instances they are rejected from entering and fled from.

Another depiction of windows that is present in both works is the portrayal of the window as a means of discovery, revealing to characters that which can be seen through the window. As with windows as a physical barrier, this may seem a self-evident purpose for a window to serve, however, when one considers that the significant revelations of both books are uncovered by gazing through a window, it becomes apparent that windows are important vehicles for each narrative. Throughout *Wuthering Heights*, characters gaze and spy through windows, open windows, and break them. Not surprisingly, the large drawing-room window of Thrushcross Grange appears ample and cheery compared to windows at Wuthering Heights. Rather than being 'narrow' and 'deeply set' it provides accessible views out onto the garden and green valley and, conversely, into the home's interior. When Catherine and Heathcliff venture out to spy on Edgar and Isabella, the drawing-room window provides a view into a different world—one that eventually welcomes Catherine but rejects Heathcliff. Thrown out of Thrushcross Grange (as he will be many more times), Heathcliff is left to make his observations through the glass partition: 'I resumed my station as a spy, because, if Catherine had wished to return, I intended shattering their great glass panes to a million fragments unless they let her out.' When Catherine falls ill, Heathcliff asks the maidservant, Nelly Dean, to ask for permission to visit, and he says he will wait in the garden until he gets a reply. When Catherine dies, the stories narrator and servant, Nelly Dean, goes out to the group of larch trees by the house where Heathcliff had spent the night. Nelly goes to tell him of her death but Heathcliff already knows, having watched through the windows the night before.

Both novels are punctuated with death, and often this is discovered through or caused by an open window. In *Frankenstein*, Victor tears apart the she-creature in front of the creature who was watching his progress on his future companion's creation through the window, outside. Often windows are described as being a figurative reflection of something and in this scene (which takes place at night) they could be more about a literal reflection. When Victor looks at the window, he would have invariably seen his own face first, and then when the lightning flashed, seen the monster's own face illuminated outside in the same spot. This could have been the real reason for his disgust and horror, as in the first motion picture adaptation of Shelley's novel, where the film concludes with Victor looking into a mirror and his reflection changes into the creature. He is disgusted by the creature perhaps because he is so like a part of himself that he detests and is interchangeably connected to. Likewise, in Danny Boyle's modern theatre production, the duality of Victor and the creature was further emphasized with the two main actors having interchangeable roles as those characters.

In an act of revenge later in the novel, the tables are turned when on his honeymoon, Victor sees the creature taunting him at the open window, 'he seemed to jeer, and with his fiendish finger he pointed towards the corpse of my wife.' This direct act of revenge is even more poignant since it occurs with each separated by the window. It shows how alike Victor and his creation are, now that their roles are reversed and the creature is able to hurt and punish Victor for destroying 'the companion on which his future happiness depended.'

Windows function as a means of learning via observation in both books. Heathcliff and the creature spend large amounts of time observing their friends and loved ones through windows, and act violently in defence and retaliation when they eventually reject them. Frankenstein's creature spies on the family in the woods through a crack in the wall, which acts as his window into the world of humans and leads to his self-education. When he attempts to introduce himself to them, feeling by that time as if he was well acquainted with them, they beat him and chased him out of their house. In a literal sense, a window is simply a border between you and the outside world, through which one can look in or out. However, in these novels, windows act as a means of observing and learning about things that would be otherwise unknown. The creature in *Frankenstein* evidences this very clearly in his observation of the family in the house in the woods. Through a boarded up window he finds 'a small and almost imperceptible chink through which the eye could just penetrate', and from there he watches and teaches himself to speak from his study of them. The creature's first experience of love and care is seen between the old man and his young daughter and he is so overwhelmed by it he 'withdrew from the window, unable to bear the emotions.' This is a very significant point in the creature's narrative as the window is his only portal to them and the fact that he stepped away shows how clearly he felt the physical separation he had from them and humanity in general. He so desperately desires to love and be loved, but knows he is unable to fit into human society. In Carina Brännström's essay on alienation in *Frankenstein*, she states that 'The family symbolizes the creature's first "school" of human nature, and the lesson it learns is that it does not fit in.'

Windows in the symbolic and figurative sense also feature largely throughout the novels. The many symbolic meanings of windows extend even to appearances, as Nelly describes Heathcliff's eyes as 'a couple of black fiends, so deeply buried, who never open their windows boldly.' His eyes are later described by his wife, Isabella Linton as 'clouded windows of hell which flashed at me.' Again, windows prevent rather than provide access. It is said that 'eyes are the windows to the soul', meaning that when others engage us, despite whatever facial expressions may be employed, a glimpse of the eyes will give away the innermost feelings. Similarly in a house, the windows can represent the true feelings or intentions of a character. For instance, in *Frankenstein*, Victor is recovering from an illness brought on with the shock of creating living dead, and he contemplates nature: 'I perceived that the fallen leaves had disappeared and that the young buds were shooting forth from the trees that shaded my window.' This observation is indicative of Victor's return to peace of mind, as he is once again able to take joy in the beauty of nature, as he did prior to his obsession with bringing the creature to life.

Both Heathcliff and the creature are the characters that embody the wildness of nature in their respective stories, and their isolation from the other characters is shown through their constant placement on the other side of the windows. This means of looking in on others through the windows from outside shows how they are on the fringe of society, and more closely connected to nature than to the civilized world that the other side of the window represents. Throughout the novels, windows are able to offer a reflection of the internal situation the characters find themselves in. This perhaps is why Heathcliff and the creature identify so closely with nature, as it contains the same wild passions they themselves have. Catherine Linton, as she lay dying, 'sat in the open recess of the window' and always had the window opened so that she too could feel peace in her connection to nature through the window, and thereby a connection to her love, Heathcliff. Her servant Ellen attempts to close it, not wanting to 'give her death of a cold,' to which Catherine, tells her 'you won't give me a chance of life.' To Catherine, windows increasingly are her only connection to the unruly elements of nature and childhood that she left behind in her strategic marriage to Edgar. Her marriage was a means of upward social mobility, and so it was no longer acceptable to run amongst the moors or be alone with Heathcliff, an unmarried man of debatable character, so windows gave her a chance to feel that connection still whilst remaining indoors where she was expected to be.

Lastly, windows serve the significant purpose of providing an exit to narrative. *Frankenstein* ends with Walton confronting the creature, who had crept onto his ship in order to mourn the death of his creator, Victor. He vows to 'collect my funeral pyre and consume to ashes' his body so that no one could ever find his remains and 'create such another as I have been.' So saying 'he sprang from the cabin window…and was soon borne away by the waves and lost in the darkness and distance.' *Wuthering Heights* ends with the discovery of Heathcliff's death when a servant 'observed the master's window swinging open' during a heavy rainstorm. He is found lying on his 'rain-soaked' bed, a hand resting on the windowsill, and the servant attempts to close both 'the lattice, flapping to and fro' and the 'frightful gaze' of his eyes. In both novels, the protagonists leave their physical surroundings through the window, allowing them to not only leave behind the restrictive frames of their lives but also leave the frames of their narratives.

WITH GRACE

by Ellie Fuller (a former student)

For Liz

With deep gratitude for the doors opened, for the mentorship and understanding.

With grace she goes
across this Earth
through all life's changing faces.
Each new challenge
met square-on,
unflinching gaze wise.
Gentle, yet resolute beyond what one might know.

Thoughts spread wide
amongst myriad layers
catching strands of life;
weaving a basket of beauty.
(Just like she showed me a poem could do).
Heart open wide
to the pain and beauty of it all
always—and now even more so.
Hands gently guiding others,
catching stories,
opening doors

without noise or ask of praise.

Steady in pursuit of something that's hard to define.
Something I can wrap up in 'bringing good into this world,'
though that doesn't catch it all.
Maybe 'light', love.'..? It's something beyond
—bigger than the clichéd words it sticks at—
but it shines.
In our classroom it appeared as excitement, passion
and a little bit of magic;
a glimpse through a door she invited us to open.

She delves down, lives deep and long,

and then in a moment
life opens and spirals and connects.
A bright light in eyes focused far away
as if looking into another realm.
Aha
Oh, it's always been so. She smiles.

Clear-sighted
with vision and soul open to the more-than-visible world,
worlds beyond ours—after ours.
And always
bearing hope in her being.
You can see it if you spend an afternoon in the sun with her.
It's a quiet blue light in her eyes.

She treds lightly on this Earth,
yet flowers grow in her footsteps
where others may follow
and do.
I hope she knows
she's printed in hearts,
as with grace she goes.

NOTES

Chapter 1

1   Shakespeare, William. *A Midsummer Night's Dream*. 3.2.
2   Dormandy, Simon. *The Arts and Creativity—integrating performing arts based approaches across the curriculum.* A paper presented at Performance Arts in the Classroom (London, November 2012).
3   Robinson, Ken. *Out of Our Minds* (Capstone, London, 2011) p. 96.
4   Ibid. p. 98.
5   Ibid. p. 100.
6   Ibid. p. 178.
7   Ibid. p. 179.
8   Goethe, Johann Wolfgang. *Metamorphosis of Plants* (MIT Press, Cambridge MA, 2009) Ed. Gordon L. Miller.
9   Robinson, Ken. *Out of Our Minds* (Capstone, London, 2011) p. 190.
10 Ibid. p. 191.
11 Miller. p. xxiii.
12 Robinson, Ken. *The Element: How Finding Your Passion Changes Everything* (Penguin, London, 2009) p. 67.
13 Ibid. p. 75.
14 Ibid. p. 77.
15 Ibid. p. 79.
16 Ibid.
17 Ibid. p. 90.
18 Ibid. p. 94.
19 Ibid. p. 174.
20 Ibid. p. 179.
21 Ibid. p. 180.
22 Ibid. p. 182.
23 Ibid.
24 Ibid. p. 198.

Chapter 2

1   *The Guardian* interview, Youtube, 4 Oct 2011.
2   Arnold, Matthew. *Culture and Anarchy* (Cambridge University Press, Cambridge, 1948) p. 48.
3   Ibid. 1948 p. 48.
4   Departmental Committee of the Board of Education. *The Newbolt Report: The teaching of English in England.* (London, 1921) p. 20).

[5] Abbs, Peter. *The Arts, Postmodern Culture and Education.* (Routledge, London, 2003) p. 12.

[6] Holmes, Edmond. *What Is and What Might Be.* (Constable, London, 2011) p. 43.

[7] Ibid. p. 50.

[8] Ibid. p. 51.

[9] Ibid. p. 178.

[10] Robinson, Ken. *Out of Our Minds* (Capstone, London, 2011) p. 179.

[11] Ibid.

[12] Dewey, John. *Experience and Education* (Touchstone, New York NY, 1997) p. 25.

[13] Ibid.

[14] Ibid. p. 26.

[15] Dewey, John. *Experience and Education* (Touchstone, New York NY, 1997) p. 90.

[16] Ibid. p. 91.

[17] Steiner, Rudolf. *The Science of Knowing: Outline of an Epistemology Implicit in the Goethean World View.* (Mercury Press, Spring Valley NY, 1988) Trans. William Lindeman. p. 1.

[18] Ibid.

[19] Ibid. p. 2.

[20] Steiner, Rudolf. *Goethean Science.* (Mercury Press, Spring Valley NY, 1988) Trans. William Lindeman. p. 2.

[21] Ibid.

[22] Ibid. p. 4.

[23] Steiner, Rudolf. *The Science of Knowing: Outline of an Epistemology Implicit in the Goethean World View.* (Mercury Press, Spring Valley NY, 1988) Trans. William Lindeman. p. 3.

[24] Ibid. p. 20.

[25] Ibid. p. 21.

[26] Ibid. p. 23.

[27] Ibid. p. 33.

[28] Steiner's italics, p. 33.

[29] Ibid.

[30] Steiner's italics, p. 57.

[31] Ibid. p. 65.

[32] Lorimer, David (ed) *Thinking Beyond the Brain: A Wider Science of Consciousness* (Floris Books, Edinburgh, 2001) p. 188.

[33] Csíkszentmihályi, Mihaly. *Flow: the Classic Work on How to Achieve Happiness.* (Rider, London, 2002).

[34] Steiner, Rudolf. *The Science of Knowing: Outline of an Epistemology Implicit in the Goethean World View.* (Mercury Press, Spring Valley NY, 1988) Trans. William Lindeman. p. 59.

[35] Ibid. p. 61.

[36] Ibid. p. 62.

[37] Bruner, Jerome. *Actual Minds, Possible Worlds* (Harvard University Press, Cambridge MA, 1986) p. 4.

[38] Ibid. p. 5.

[39] Ibid. p. 11.

[40] Ibid. p. 12.

[41] Ibid. p. 13.

[42] Ibid. p. 13.

[43] Ibid. p. 18.

[44] Steiner, Rudolf. *The Science of Knowing: Outline of an Epistemology Implicit in the Goethean World View.* (Mercury Press, Spring Valley NY, 1988) Trans. William Lindeman. p. 103.

[45] Ibid. p. 60.

Chapter 3

[1] Topolinski, Sascha, & Reber, Rolf. Gaining Insight into the 'Aha'-experience. (Current Directions in Psychological Science, 2010) Vol 19. pp. 402-405.

[2] Auble, Pamela, Franks, Jefferey, & Soraci, Salvatore. (1979) *Effort toward Comprehension: Elaboration or 'Aha'?* (Memory and Cognition, 1979) Vol 7. pp 426-434.)

[3] See Clarke, Shirley, ed. *Formative Assessment in the Secondary Classroom* (Hodder Education, London, 2012.

[4] Robinson, Ken. Out of Our Minds (Capstone, London, 2011) p. 110.

[5] Ibid. p. 111.

[6] Ibid. p. 112.

[7] Ibid. p. 179.

[8] Ibid. p. 180.

[9] Ibid. p. 181.

[10] Ibid. p. 182.

[11] Ibid. p. 195.

[12] Goethe, Johann Wolfgang. *Metamorphosis of Plants* (MIT Press, Cambridge MA, 2009) Ed. Gordon L. Miller. p. 11.

[13] Ibid.

[14] Steiner, Rudolf. *Goethe's World View.* (Mercury Press, Spring Valley NY, 1985) Trans. William Lindeman. p. 6.

[15] Steiner, Rudolf. *The Philosophy of Freedom: The Basis for a Modern World Conception,* (Rudolf Steiner Press, London, 1963) p. 24.

[16] My italics, Introduction p. 24.

[17] Ibid. p. 65.

[18] Ibid. pp. 65-66.

[19] Seamon, David and Zajonc, Arthur, ed. *Goethe's Way of Science: A Phenomenology of Nature* (SUNY, Albany NY, 1998).

[20] Ibid. p. 263.

[21] Ibid. p. 264.

[22] Ibid.

[23] Petty, Geoffrey. *Teaching Today* (Nelson Thornes, Cheltenham, 2009) and Petty, Geoffrey. *Evidence-based Teaching* (Nelson Thornes, Cheltenham, 2009).

[24] Clarke, Shirley. *Active Learning Through Formative Assessment* (Hodder Education, London, 2012). My italics.

Chapter 4

[1] Recollection from Caroline von Heydebrand of Rudolf Steiner's introductory remarks opening the Study of Man conference, 21 August, 1919.

[2] Diary entry 27 September 2012.

[3] *Discovering the Etheric Heart*, by Liz Attwell, Michael Hall, 2012, from Rudolf Steiner *The Human Heart*, lecture on 26 May, 1922, GA212, Spring Valley, New York: Mercury Press, 1985. And in *Life of the Human Soul, Lecture 6*, pp. 87-101— Followed by Steiner's diagrams in *Life of the Human Soul, Lecture 6*, p. 90 and p. 91.

[4] Diary entry referring to Steiner's *Life of the Human Soul and its Relation to World Evolution*, Lecture 4 pp.56-60. Followed by Steiner's diagram from Ibid. p. 57.

[5] Liz's reference to *The Ninth Century and the Holy Grail, W.J. Stein Preface p. xii.*

[6] *Parzival*, Book 5, p. 99 in Walter Johannes Stein, Temple Lodge Press 1988 (published in German in 1928).

[7] Here she names 'the loftiest planet' Saturn, Jupiter, Mars and Sun, 'point to good fortune in you'; Venus, Mercury and 'the nearest to us,' Moon.

[8] *Parzival*, Book 15, Hatto trans, Penguin Books, 1980, pp. 387-388.

[9] *Medieval English Lyrics*, ed. R.T. Davies, Faber, 1963; pp. 160-161.

[10] From *Educating the Adolescent: Discipline or Freedom*, Erich Gabert, 1928, trans by Ruth Pusch, Anthroposophic Press, N.Y. 1987.

[11] *Paradise Lost*, John Milton, *Book XII, 645-end.*

[12] *Liz's Diary*, 1 Oct 2012; quoting from Naydler in *New View*.

[13] Notes LA/JA 31 July 2019.

[14] Shakespeare, *Twelfth Night*, I.i.9-15.

[15] *Twelfth Night*, V.i.378.

[16] Liz quoting Richard Bunzl, in her Diary, 1 Oct 2012.

[17] from Alwyn, Josie and Masters, Brien. *Educating the Soul* (Temple Lodge, Forest Row 2016) pp. 6-7.

Learning is a life process.

The discovery that the journey of Shakespeare's creative life and the evolutionary journey of adolescent consciousness run parallel leads to an essential understanding of the educational process at any stage of human life. Learning is a narrative process and each learning process also follows the same transformative course as the fundamental processes of life—whether it is the process of breathing, of digesting, of learning, of creating, or the process of the whole human life. Whether the process is macrocosmic or microcosmic, each time it will follow the paradigmatic sevenfold life-process. This understanding enables us to take one further step in discovering how it is that Shakespeare's plays can so engage their audience to bring about a transformative education for the soul. It is the understanding that the human soul is an organism designed for transforming consciousness, and it is demonstrated in work by Baruch Urieli and Hans Müller-Wiedemann, and of Liz Attwell, on looking into the etheric realm. These authors use the example of how the human eye perceives colour to demonstrate, metonymically, the activity of the whole human organism... [See Chapter Three, 'A Dynamic Analogy,' p. 45, describing how the after-image of a primary colour is a complementary colour].

From this demonstration we may see that the human being is naturally predisposed to complement and inwardly complete what is perceived as incomplete in the outer, sense-perceptible world: 'Thus the world of the senses does not stand in contrast to the world of the spirit which it has lost but forms an indivisible unity with it, which remains hidden until the selfless self has learnt once again to perceive the spiritual two thirds missing from the earthly percept. In this way, it becomes possible for man to unveil the true meaning of existence...' (Urieli). Eurythmists, for example, understand and work with this inner 'completing activity' of the soul, taking account in their performances that their audience, though outwardly sitting still, are inwardly 'moving eurythmically' in response to the entire experience of the on-stage performance. This adds an extra dimension to conscious artistic work. .

18 Diary, 23 December 2012 .

19 Rudolf Steiner, 1907, in Diary, 27 December 2012.

20 Diary, 27 October 2012.

21 Rudolf Steiner, Ibid. p. 37; in Diary, 15 November 2012.

22 From a filmed conversation with Catherine Fenton.

23 Diary, 3 October 2012.

24 Diary, 31 October 2012.

25 Rudolf Steiner, *Goethean Science*, p. 27.

26 Diary, 31 October 2012.

27 *New Statesman* review, epigraph to *The Subtle Knife*, vol. 2. *His Dark Materials*, pub Scholastic UK, 1997.

28 Five volumes out of the six planned, published between the 1990s and the 2020s.

29 From Pullman, Philip. *The Subtle Knife* (Scholastic London 2011 ed.) p.90-6 [italics editor's own]:

'Lyra looked. The glass was dark and blank. She saw her own reflection dimly, but that was all. As an experiment she pretended that she was reading the alethiometer, and imagined herself asking: What does this woman know about Dust? What questions is *she* asking? .

She mentally moved the alethiometer's hands around the dial, and as she did, the screen began to flicker. Astonished, she came out of her concentration, and the flicker died. She didn't notice the ripple of excitement that made Dr Malone sit up: she frowned and sat forward and began to concentrate again.

This time the response came instantaneously. A stream of dancing lights, for all the world like the shimmering curtains of the aurora, blazed across the screen. They took up patterns that were held for a moment only to break apart and form again, in different shapes, or different colours; they looped and swayed, they sprayed apart, they burst into showers of radiance that suddenly swerved this way or that like a flock of birds changing direction in the sky. And as Lyra watched, she felt the same sense, as of *trembling on the brink of understanding*, that she remembered from the time when she was beginning to read the alethiometer. She asked another question: Is *this* Dust? Is it the same thing making these patterns and moving the needle of the alethiometer? .

The answer came in more loops and swirls of light. She guessed it meant yes. [...].

And she turned back and focused her mind again, but this time she pretended to herself that the screen was the alethiometer, with all thirty-six symbols laid out round the edge. She knew them so well now that her fingers automatically twisted in her lap as she moved the imaginary hands to point at the candle (for understanding), the alpha and omega (for language), and the ant (for diligence), and framed the question: What would these people have to do in order to understand the language of the Shadows?

The screen responded as quickly as thought itself, and out of the welter of lines and flashes a series of pictures formed with perfect clarity: compasses, alpha and omega again, lightning, angel. Each picture flashed up a different number of times, and then came a different three: camel, garden, moon.

Lyra saw their meanings clearly, and unfocused her mind to explain. This time, when she turned around, she saw that Dr Malone was sitting back in her chair, white-faced, clutching the edge of the table.

"What it says," Lyra told her, "it's saying in my language, right, the language of pictures. Like the alethiometer. But what it says is that it could use ordinary language too, words, if you fixed it up like that. You could fix this so it put words on the screen. But you'd need a lot of careful figuring with numbers—that was the compasses, see—and the lightning meant anbaric, I mean electric power, more of that. And the angel—that's all about messages. There's things it wants to say. But when it went on to that second bit.. It meant Asia, almost the furthest east but not quite. I dunno what country that would be—China, maybe.. And there's a way they have in that country of talking to Dust, I mean Shadows, same as you got here and I got with the—I got with pictures, only their way uses sticks. […] but I didn't understand it really. I thought when I first saw it there was something important about it, only I didn't know what. So there must be lots of ways of talking to Shadows." […]   "So anyway," she said, "you could make this screen so it could talk to you in words, if you wanted. Then you could talk to the Shadows like I talk to the alethiometer. But what I want to know is, why do the people in my world hate it? Dust, I mean, Shadows. Dark matter. They want to destroy it. They think it's evil. But I think what *they* do is evil. I seen them do it. So what is it, Shadows? Is it good or evil, or what?".

Dr Malone rubbed her face and made her cheeks even redder than they were. .

"Everything about this is *embarrassing*,' she said. 'D'you know how embarrassing it is to mention good and evil in a scientific laboratory? Have you any idea? One of the reasons I became a scientist was not to have to think about that kind of thing."

"You *got* to think about it," said Lyra severely. 'You can't investigate Shadows, Dust, whatever it is, without thinking about that kind of thing, good and evil and such. And it said you got to remember. You can't refuse."

30 Ibid. p.87.

31 Ibid. p.94.

32 Ibid. p. 96.

33 Ibid. p. 96.

34 *The Amber Spyglass,* vol 3, *His Dark Materials by Philip Pullman.*

35 Preface to *The Secret Commonwealth*, vol. 2. *Book of Dust*, David Fickling Books, Oxford, 2019.

36 Preface to *The Subtle Knife.*

37 'We call it the Cave. Shadows on the walls of the cave, you see, from Plato.' pp. 88-9.

38 Philip Pullman, *The Book of Dust*, Vol 1. La Belle Sauvage. pp. 204-8.

39 Leader of the Pedagogical Section at the Goetheanum.

40 See Steiner, *The Philosophy of Freedom.*

41 Lecturing at a Steiner Education Conference in Denmark at which Liz was a UK SWSF delegate.

42 Incidentally, or perhaps not, tremendous has its roots in the Latin *'tremere'* to tremble'.

43 See Rudolf Steiner, Eurythmy First Course (20 September 1912).

44 Rudolf Steiner, *Life of the Human Soul*, Dornach, 29 April to 17 June 1922. Rudolf Steiner, *The Riddle of Humanity*, Lecture 8, 13 August 1916 and Lecture 9, 15 August 1916.

45 From van Houten, Coenraad. *Awakening the Will* (Temple Lodge, Forest Row, 2003) pp. 44-7.

46 Josie Alwyn/Liz Attwell conversation. Notes from 31 July 2019.

[47] Liz notes in her Diary on 23 Dec 2012: 'I have come into the presence of the Grail'.

[48] Rudolf Steiner's drawing of the Seventh Seal and painting by Clara Rettich based on Rudolf Steiner's design. See *Rosicrusianism Renewed* (CW284)—ref. in *The Rose Cross Meditation*, p. 13.

[49] As in, for example, R. Steiner, *Occult Science*, ch. 5.

[50] Examples that demonstrate this, such the essays by Laura Manning and India Ashe, are included in the appendices to this book.

[51] see *Occult Science* ch. 5, p. 255.

[52] R. Steiner, *How can Man find the Christ Again?*.

[53] R. Steiner, *Goethean Science*, p. 27; in Diary 31, Oct 2012.

[54] R. Steiner, *The Rose Cross Meditation: an archetype of human development*, 2016. p. 26.

[55] Liz Attwell, a written postscript to the Whitsun Address she gave at Emerson College, Sussex, UK, summer 2019.

[56] Liz Attwell, speaking with Josie Alwyn, summer 2019.

BIBLIOGRAPHY

Chapter One

Daily Telegraph, 23.04.11.

Dormandy, Simon. *The Arts and Creativity—integrating performing arts based approaches across the curriculum.* A paper presented at Performance Arts in the Classroom (London, November 2012).

Goethe, Johann Wolfgang. *Metamorphosis of Plants* (MIT Press, Cambridge MA, 2009) Ed. Gordon L. Miller.

Goethe, Johann Wolfgang. *Theory of Colours* (Dover Publications, New York NY, 2006).

National Advisory Committee on Creative and Cultural Education. *All Our Futures.* (Department for Education and Employment, London, 1999).

Robinson, Ken. *Out of Our Minds* (Capstone, London, 2011).

Robinson, Ken. *The Element* (Penguin, London, 2009).

Rudolf, Steiner. *Goethe's World View* (Mercury Press, Spring Valley NY, 1985) Trans. William Lindeman.

Rudolf, Steiner. *The Science of Knowing: Outline of an Epistemology Implicit in the Goethean World View.* (Mercury Press, Spring Valley NY, 1988) Trans. William Lindeman.

Shakespeare, William. *A Midsummer Night's Dream.*

Chapter Two

Abbs, Peter. *The Arts, Postmodern Culture and Education.* (Routledge, London, 2003).

Arnold, Matthew. *Culture and Anarchy* (Cambridge University Press, Cambridge, 1948).

Butterworth, Jez. *Jerusalem* (Oberon Books, London, 2010).

Bruner, Jerome. *Actual Minds, Possible Worlds* (Harvard University Press, Cambridge MA, 1986).

Csíkszentmihályi, Mihaly. *Flow: the Classic Work on How to Achieve Happiness.* (Rider, London, 2002).

Departmental Committee of the Board of Education. *The Newbolt Report: The teaching of English in England* (London, 1921).

Dewey, John. *Experience and Education* (Touchstone, New York NY, 1997).

Goethe, Johann Wolfgang. *Metamorphosis of Plants* (MIT Press, Cambridge MA, 2009) Ed. Gordon L. Miller.

Holmes, Edmond. *What Is and What Might Be* (Constable, London, 2011).

Lorimer, David (ed) *Thinking Beyond the Brain: A Wider Science of Consciousness* (Floris Books, Edinburgh, 2001).

Marshall, Bethan. *English Teachers—the Unofficial Guide: researching the philosophies of English teachers* (Routledge Falmer, London, 2000).

'Playwright Jez Butterworth on Jerusalem, England and Englishness' (*The Guardian* interview, Youtube, 4 Oct 2011).

Robinson, Ken. *Out of Our Minds* (Capstone, London, 2011).

Steiner, Rudolf. *The Science of Knowing: Outline of an Epistemology Implicit in the Goethean World View.* (Mercury Press, Spring Valley NY, 1988) Trans. William Lindeman.

Steiner, Rudolf. *Goethean Science.* (Mercury Press, Spring Valley NY, 1988) Trans. William Lindeman.

The Times, 'Letters' (London, 1 October 2013).

Chapter Three

Auble, Pamela, Franks, Jefferey, & Soraci, Salvatore. *Effort toward Comprehension: Elaboration or 'Aha'?* (Memory and Cognition, 1979) Vol 7. pp 426-434.

Clarke, Shirley, ed. *Formative Assessment in the Secondary Classroom* (Hodder Education, London, 2012).

Clarke, Shirley. *Active Learning Through Formative Assessment* (Hodder Education, London, 2012).

Goethe, Johann Wolfgang. *Metamorphosis of Plants* (MIT Press, Cambridge MA, 2009).

Hougham, Paul. *Dialogues of Destiny: A Postmodern Appreciation of Waldorf Education* (Sylvan Associates, Malvern Hills, 2013).

Petty, Geoffrey. *Teaching Today* (Nelson Thornes, Cheltenham, 2009).

Petty, Geoffrey. *Evidence-based Teaching* (Nelson Thornes, Cheltenham, 2009).

Robinson, Ken. *Out of Our Minds* (Capstone, London, 2011).

Seamon, David and Zajonc, Arthur, ed. *Goethe's Way of Science: A Phenomenology of Nature* (State University of New York Press, Albany NY, 1998).

Steiner, Rudolf. *The Science of Knowing: Outline of an Epistemology Implicit in the Goethean World View.* (Mercury Press, Spring Valley NY, 1988) Trans. William Lindeman.

Steiner, Rudolf. *Goethe's World View.* (Mercury Press, Spring Valley NY, 1985) Trans. William Lindeman.

Steiner, Rudolf. *The Philosophy of Freedom:* The Basis for a Modern World Conception (Rudolf Steiner Press, London, 1963).

The Times, 'Lives were ruined by child-led learning, says Ofsted Chief' (London, 22 March 2014).

Topolinski, Sascha, & Reber, Rolf. *Gaining Insight into the 'Aha'-experience*. (Current Directions in Psychological Science, 2010) Vol 19. pp. 402-405.

Chapter Four

Rudolf Steiner:

The Education of the Child

Eurythmy First Course (5th Day, 20 September 1912)

Goethean Science

Heart Thinking: Inspired Knowledge by Rudolf Steiner; selected and compiled by Martina Maria Sam; trans. Matthew Barton; Rudolf Steiner Press, 2017.

How can Man find the Christ Again?, specifically Lecture 5, 28th December, 1918.

The Human Heart, lecture on May 26, 1922, GA212 (Mercury Press, Spring Valley NY, 1985.

Imagination: Enhancing the Powers of Thinking (Rudolf Steiner Press, 2019) compiled and edited by Edward de Boer; trans. Matthew Barton.

Intuition: The Focus of Thinking (Rudolf Steiner Press, 2019) Ed. Edward de Boer; Trans. J. Collis.

Knowledge of Higher Worlds

Life of the Human Soul and its Relation to World Evolution. Dornach, 29 April to 17 June 1922.

Occult Science

Philosophy of Freedom

The Riddle of Humanity, August, 1916.

The Rose Cross Meditation: an Archetype of Human Development (Rudolf Steiner Press, 2016) Trans. Johanna Collis.

Study of Man (Foundations of Human Experience) August 21, 1919.

Other writers on the theme:

Alwyn, Josie and Masters, Brien. *Educating the Soul* (Temple Lodge, Forest Row 2016).

Davies, R.T. ed. *Medieval English Lyrics* (Faber,1963).

Gabert, Erich. *Educating the Adolescent: Discipline or Freedom* (Anthroposophic Press, N.Y., 1987) Trans. Ruth Pusch.

Hatto, A.T. trans. *Parzival* (Penguin Books, London, 1980).

Houten, Coenraad van. *Awakening the Will* (Temple Lodge, Forest Row, 2003).

Leiber, Elan. ed. *Entry Points; A Guide to Rudolf Steiner's Study of Man* (Pedagogical Section Council of North America, 2017).

John Milton. *Paradise Lost.*

Pullman, Philip. *The Subtle Knife*, vol. 2. *His Dark Materials* (Scholastic UK, London, 1997).

Pullman, Philip. *The Amber Spyglass,* vol. 3. *His Dark Materials* (Scholastic UK, London, 2000).

Pullman, Philip. *The Secret Commonwealth*, vol 2. *Book of Dust* (David Fickling Books, Oxford, 2019).

Philip Pullman, *The Book of Dust*, vol. 1. *La Belle Sauvage* (David Fickling Books, Oxford, 2017).

Shakespeare, William. *Twelfth Night.*

Shakespeare, William. *Hamlet.*

Stein, Walter Johannes. *The Ninth Century and the Holy Grail* (Temple Lodge Press, Forest Row, 1988) First published in German in 1928.

Specifically recommended for reference to Steiner's work on the theme of Chapter 4:

Heart Thinking: Inspired Knowledge by Rudolf Steiner; (Rudolf Steiner Press, 2017) Compiled Martina Maria Sam; Trans. Matthew Barton.

How can Man find the Christ Again?, in particular Lecture 5, 28 December, 1918.

Imagination: Enhancing the Powers of Thinking (Rudolf Steiner Press, 2019) compiled and edited by Edward de Boer; trans. Matthew Barton.

Intuition: The Focus of Thinking (Rudolf Steiner Press, 2019) Ed. Edward de Boer; Trans. J. Collis.

The Riddle of Humanity, in particular Lectures 8 and 9, August 13-15, 1916.

The Rose Cross Meditation: an Archetype of Human Development (Rudolf Steiner Press, 2016) Trans. Johanna Collis.

Part Two

Clarke, Shirley, ed. *Formative Assessment in the Secondary Classroom* (Hodder Education, London, 2012).

Clarke, Shirley. *Active Learning Through Formative Assessment* (Hodder Education, London, 2012).

Clouder, Christopher and Mitchell, David. *Rudolf Steiner's Observations on Adolescence: The Third Phase of Human Development* (AWSNA Publications, Hudson NY, 2001).

Robb, Marina, Richardson, Anna and Mew, Victoria. *Learning with Nature: A How To Guide to Inspiring Children Through Outdoor Games and Activities* (Green Books, Cambridge, 2015).

Steiner, Rudolf. *Education for Adolescents: Eight Lectures* (Anthroposophic Press, Hudson NY, 1996) Trans. Carl Hoffmann.

Appendix 2

Mary Shelley. *Frankenstein*. 1818.

Emily Brontë. *Wuthering Heights*. 1847.

Carina Brännström. *An Analysis of the Theme of Alienation in Mary Shelley's Frankenstein*. Academic essay for Luleå University of Technology, Department of Language and Culture, 2006.

Thomas A. Edison film. *Frankenstein*. Directed by J. Searle Dawley, 1910.

Danny Boyle, dir. National Theatre production. *Frankenstein—The Modern Myth*. 2012.

Online Resources

https://www.shirleyclarke-education.org/

https://redsquirrelresources.co.uk/

For further information and resources, visit www.lizattwell.co.uk (with thanks to Rollo Attwell).

Steiner

A NOTE FROM RUDOLF STEINER PRESS

We are an independent publisher and registered charity (non-profit organisation) dedicated to making available the work of Rudolf Steiner in English translation. We care a great deal about the content of our books and have hundreds of titles available – as printed books, ebooks and in audio formats.

As a publisher devoted to anthroposophy…

- We continually commission translations of previously unpublished works by Rudolf Steiner and invest in re-translating, editing and improving our editions.

- We are committed to making anthroposophy available to all by publishing introductory books as well as contemporary research.

- Our new print editions and ebooks are carefully checked and proofread for accuracy, and converted into all formats for all platforms.

- Our translations are officially authorised by Rudolf Steiner's estate in Dornach, Switzerland, to whom we pay royalties on sales, thus assisting their critical work.

So, look out for Rudolf Steiner Press as a mark of quality and support us today by buying our books, or contact us should you wish to sponsor specific titles or to support the charity with a gift or legacy.

office@rudolfsteinerpress.com
Join our e-mailing list at www.rudolfsteinerpress.com

RUDOLF STEINER PRESS